How to make fear your ally

Go deeply in yourself before overcoming what you are afraid of

By Emil Howthorn

Table of Contents

Chapter 1: What is fear, anyway?

Fear is one of the seven common feelings that everyone around the world has felt. Fear comes with the real or imagined threat of harm, physical, emotional, or psychological. Although traditionally considered a negative emotion, fear actually serves an important role in keeping us safe as it mobilizes us to cope with potential hazards: what is fear? Defining what fear is not may be helpful at first.

Fear is a primary feeling that occurs when we feel threatened. It's sensitive to fear. It's supposed to protect us. Fear comes from an ancient part of our brain that developed to keep our ancestors protected from talking in the bush from tigers. This is why fear can have physical symptoms such as sweaty hands and a higher heart rate, also known as the condition of fight or flight. We need to act quickly when we come across a tiger in the bush to survive.

And while fear is indeed an ally when it comes to keeping us safe, what often happens is that events that aren't as dangerous as walking in the bush by a tiger trigger our response to fight or flight. The anxiety is heightened when we are under excessive stress or persistent overwhelming. We can easily be afraid of just about any or all future events at low level.

What if you fail, what if you get killed, what if you think you're dumb, what if you lose money, what if you say no, what if you say yes?

All those, if not actual events, but something that we are projecting into the future. And when you start something different, whether it's a pivot with your career or company, a new project, or a transfer, you may be distracted by too much of that.

Everyone can be scared; fear is a facet of human experience that is inevitable.

People usually see fear as an unpleasant emotion, but some go out of their way to trigger it such as jumping off planes or watching scary films.

Fear is justifiable; for example, when you know that you are the only home, hearing footsteps inside your house is a valid reason to be frightened.

Fear may also be inappropriate; for instance, when watching a sliced film, we might feel a rush of fear, even though we know the creature is an actor in makeup and the blood is not real.

Some people consider phobias to be the most dangerous type of terror. They can attach to almost anything like spiders, clowns, paper, or carpets and have a significant impact on the lives of people.

You should not promote blind optimism or decision-making without taking into account the specifics of a specific situation. But too much fear can prevent us from moving forward, mainly unrecognized fear. It can discourage us from making our best choices, and it certainly makes the trip more challenging to enjoy along the way.

It can take a lot of shapes. In some situations, we don't feel as much anxiety as we think about experiencing in the future feelings like embarrassment or discomfort.

Fear is not an emotion of pleasure. Fear is no warmth, nourishment, relief, or reassurance. When it comes to fear, what we can all agree on is: it's distressing. It's uncomfortable, and we're just trying to navigate our way back out again a lot of the time we're in a state of fear.

Impairment in the ability to detect other feelings, such as fear, is associated with various disorders and follows over time a pattern of inter-individual variation and intra-individual stability. Deficits in the perception of fear are often associated with social and interpersonal problems, but it is not well known the mechanisms by which this cognitive deficiency may occur. One possible tool through which impaired fear identification can affect social skills is the ability to understand and acknowledge another person's point of view through reduced perspective-taking. In the current study, we hypothesized that within a well-characterized, non-clinical adult sample, intra-individual variation in the accuracy of facial emotion detection is correlated with perspective-taking skills.

Results indicated that, consistent with initial expectations, the capacity to reliably identify fear in others ' faces were positively correlated with perspective-taking. The relationship tended to be exceptional in recognizing fear, as perspective-taking was not associated substantially with understanding the other basic emotions. Results from this analysis are an initial step towards developing a possible connection between specific FER processes and difficulties in taking perspective. In a non-clinical adult sample, it is essential to establish the relationship between these processes so that we can consider the possibility of an impoverished perspective-taking developmental or pathological effect on the perception of fear.

A definition of fear could be organized around the most common physical and emotional manifestations of fear:

Increased heart rate

Sweaty palms

Trembling

Stomach butterflies

Shortness of breath

Sensation of anxiety or fear

Sensation of powerlessness

Sensation of depression or hopelessness.

Who makes us frightened?

To fear, the fundamental cause is the real or imagined risk of harm. It may be a danger to our physical, emotional, and psychological well-being. While in most of us, certain things cause fear, we can learn to be scared of almost anything.

Common fear triggers:

• Darkness or lack of immediate vision

• Heights and flight • Social contact and rejection

• Snakes, rats, spiders, and other animals

• Death and dying

Moods and Disorders:

Persistent fear can sometimes be called anxiety if we are continually worried without knowing why. The inability to recognize the trigger prevents us from removing ourselves from the situation, or the actual threat.

While fear is a common experience for many people, when it is chronic, persistent, severe, and interferes with the basic life tasks such as work and sleep, it can be considered a disorder.

1.1 Types of fear

An irrational fear of anything that is unlikely to cause harm is a phobia. The word itself is derived from the Greek word Phobos, meaning terror or horror.

For example, hydrophobia literally translates into fear of water.

People experience intense fear of an event or circumstance when someone has a phobia. Phobias are different from regular fears because they cause considerable anxiety, likely interfering with home, work, or school life.

People with phobia actively avoid or endure the phobic object or situation in intense fear or anxiety.

Phobias are a form of syndrome of anxiety. Disorders of anxiety are widespread. At some point in their lives, they are estimated to affect more than 30 percent of U.S. adults.

The American Psychiatric Association identifies several of the most common phobias in the Diagnostic and Statistical Manual of Mental Disorders, Fifth Edition (DSM-5).

Agoraphobia, a fear of locations or circumstances that cause fear or helplessness, is defined with its own special diagnosis as a particularly common fear. There is also a unique diagnosis of social phobias, which are fears related to social situations.

Specific phobias are a wide range of specific phobias related to particular artifacts and circumstances. An estimated 12.5 percent of American adults are affected by specific phobias.

Phobias are found in all shapes and sizes. Because there are an infinite number of things and conditions, there is quite a long list of common phobias.

According to DSM, specific phobias typically fall into five general categories:

- Animal-related fears (spiders, dogs, and insects)

- Natural environment-related fears (heights, thunder, darkness)

- Blood-related fears, injury, or medical problems (injections, broken bones, falls)

- Specific situations (flying, elevator riding, driving)

• Other (choking, loud noise)

There is no official phobias list beyond what is outlined in the DSM, but clinicians and researchers are making names for them as the need arises. Typically, this is achieved by combining a Greek (or sometimes Latin) prefix defining the phobia with the suffix of –phobia.

For example, by combining hydro (rain) and phobia (fear) fear of water would be called hydrophobia.

Such a phenomenon as fear of terror (phobophobia) also exists.

In fact, this is more common than you could imagine.

Often people with anxiety disorders experience panic attacks when they are in certain circumstances. Such panic attacks can be so painful that in the future, people will do their best to stop them.

Of example, if you have a panic attack while sailing, in the future you may be afraid of sailing, but you may also be afraid of panic attacks or fear hydrophobia.

Common list of phobias

It is a complicated process to research common phobias. For these disorders, most people are not seeking treatment, and cases are mostly unreported.

Such phobias often differ based on age, race, and cultural experiences.

A 1998 study of more than 8,000 respondents published in the British Journal of Psychiatry Trusted Source found that some of the most common phobias included:

acrophobia, fear of heights

aerophobia, fear of flying

arachnophobia, fear of spiders

astraphobia, fear of thunder and lightning

auto phobia, fear of being alone

claustrophobia, fear of enclosed or cramped spaces

homophobia, fear of blood

hydrophobia, fear of water

ophidio phobia, fear of snakes

zoophobia, fear of animals

Unique phobias

It tends to be incredibly specific for specific phobias. Perhaps so much that only a handful of people can be affected at a time.

These are hard to identify because most people are not disclosing their doctor's uncommon fears.

Sources of some of the more extreme phobias include:

- alectorophobia, chickens fear
- onomatophobia, naming fear
- pogonophobia, beard fear
- nephophobia, cloud fear
- cryophobia, ice, or cold fear.

1.2 Effects of Fear

Fear is a perceived threat that triggers human emotion. It is a primary survival mechanism that signals with a fight or flight response to our bodies to respond to danger. As such, keeping us safe is an essential part.

Nonetheless, when people live in constant fear, whether from their environment's physical hazards or observed threats, they may become disabled.

Fear is training us to respond to danger as fear works.

When we sense a potential hazard, our body releases hormones which:

Slow or shut down functions that are not required for survival (such as our digestive system)

Sharpening functions that may enable us to survive (such as vision). Our heart rate is rising, and blood is pumping into the muscles so that we can run faster.

Our body also increases the release of hormones into the brain area known as the amygdala to help us concentrate on the risk and keep it in our mind.

Chronic fear affects Living under constant threat has severe health effects.

Physical health: our immune system is compromised by fear and can cause cardiovascular damage, digestive problems like ulcers and irritable bowel syndrome, and reduced fertility. It can result in accelerated aging and even death premature.

Memory: Anxiety can affect long-term memory development and cause damage to some parts of the brain, such as the hippocampus. It can make it even harder to control fear, and most of the time, it can leave a person nervous. The world looks scary to someone in chronic fear, and their memories confirm that.

Brain processing and reactivity: Fear can disrupt processes in our brains that enable us to control emotions, interpret non-verbal signals and other information presented to us, evaluate and act ethically before acting. This has a negative impact on our thought and decision making, leaving us vulnerable to intense emotions and impulsive reactions. All these effects could leave us unable to act properly.

Mental health: Fatigue, clinical depression and PSTD are other long-term effects of anxiety.

Positive effects

We tend to reject fear as a weakness, but it's not that easy. It has come to understand fear as incredibly useful over the years, and here are some of the things you should have learned.

1. It goes hand in hand with courage and fear.

We use to think that when they choose to do something, we'd be afraid to do, people are courageous. We're mistaken. We could only be bold to do things that they were scared to do. In the lack of trepidation, courage does not occur.

We wrongly attributed bravery to others who wanted us to have the same. What we once failed to see was that we had the one need for courage a fear that we could meet head-on. We've come to realize that fear doesn't deny bravery. It's a tip.

2. It can be confusing for physiology.

In the end, fear is meant to keep us free. Many people are familiar with the response of battle or flight. If our lives are threatened, we are secured by physiology. For self-preservation, we are hardwired.

Sadly, in new yet non-threatening circumstances, we may also feel a similar reaction. Issues that we find uncomfortable put us on alert as well. The response is just as intense for some, while others are experiencing an attenuated version.

We always cross our signs and respond with the same enthusiasm to alter as something that has the power to destroy us. Adrenaline is not still about fighting or running, which brings us to the third point.

3. Fear is enlightening.

Fear is useful in a very different way when we have learned that life is not in danger.

We also get used to our way of being even though it's a life that's less than the one we want. For a variety of reasons, we restrict ourselves, real or imagined.

At the root, a close examination of many of these factors has fear. Personal growth involves expansion, which can be terrifying. Whether you want to be more open, more caring, or more financially stable, you will need to change your attitude and crack barriers that have already been formed.

Fear also directs us to areas in these cases that need to be explored more closely. While our instinct may be to run, guidance is much-needed for this form of terror.

To conclude, fear is not a problem itself. The issue is our response to our fears. We lose the task of deciphering the message sent to us by making fear an adversary. We gain a lot more when we choose to make it an ally.

It may paralyze us, or we can choose to process it. If the former is your approach, then it is desirable to be fearless. On the other side, who needs fearlessness if you actively choose to process?

Negative effects

We are inundated with messages of terror from our televisions to our political conversations. We are now feeling more scared of the world and our neighbors than we have in decades. But it's not all right for us to fear. Yes, according to psychology, we are being destroyed by terror.

Top of all, fear is "a chain reaction in the brain, "Fear starts with a frightening stimulus and ends with your body, preparing to shield itself from danger. It works like this: you are afraid, like seeing a cockroach, hearing a door slam in an empty apartment, or having a knife pushed into your throat.

As helpful as that response is, it can be detrimental to speed and thoroughness. "Once the fear receptors are ramped up, the brain short circuits more logical thinking routes and respond automatically to stimuli from the amygdale, according to studies from the University of Minnesota. When in this overactive state, the brain perceives experiences as unpleasant and remembers them that way. "That's unfortunate because the brain retains all the information of that particular experience time of day, pictures, sounds, tastes, weather, etc. in your long-term memory. While that makes the memory" extremely robust, it may also be distorted, "triggering the full range of physical and emotional responses. It is what is known as "fear conditioning," as the researchers explain: later, the event's sights, sounds, and other contextual information can become self-stimulus and cause fear. They may bring back the memory of the frightening incident, or they may cause us to be afraid without knowing why. Because these signs are correlated with the previous risk, they may be perceived by the brain as a danger indicator.

Although your memory and your perception of reality can play tricks with fear, it also affects your body. Fear can weaken long-term memory creation and damage the hippocampus, shorten the paths of response and cause constant anxiety feelings. Anxiety can also have long-term effects on our health, including "fatigue, chronic depression, accelerated aging and even premature death," again, according to the University of Minnesota. And that's just the beginning of their bad news: to someone in constant anxiety, the world looks frightening, and their memories reinforce that. Once the amygdale achieves this, the memory of fear is rewritten.

Distinguish between negative and positive fear.

The more positively you view the fear that you experience, the more you can appreciate the wonder that will enrich your soul and help you conquer negative fear. Every time you're scared, you can ask yourself:

1. Are you afraid of this? Worry is the main sign that you face negative fear. Worrying never contributes to a positive outcome; the time and energy are wasted. If the fear that you feel makes you anxious, you can be sure that it is not worth dwelling on that fear. Instead, turn your worry into prayer, for prayer has the power to change the situation for the better. Each time you are conscious of a disturbing thought in your mind, try to pray. It will become a habit over time that will serve you well.

2. What's behind this mystery? Figuring out how a scary thing causes a desire to learn more within you will show how it can be linked to wonder. Frequently, fear of the unknown is at the heart of anxiety. If you're worried that something is enigmatic to you, don't stop there. Decide to find out more about it. Trying out the mystery will lead you to some wonderful discoveries that expand your mind and reinforce your confidence.

3. Is that pushing you to take risks? Negative fear will discourage you from taking risks, while optimistic fear will make you uncomfortable with the status quo and will drive you out of your comfort zone. Fear is useful when you are forced to embark on adventures that will help you to learn and grow.

4. Is this an amazing thing for you? Feeling so afraid that the size of the situation will overtake you means it's bigger than you. While it may be too much for you to cope with on your own, with God's love and caring for people, including family and friends, it is possible to deal with any circumstance. Reaching for support will lessen the anxiety that you feel as the path forward becomes more transparent, and you encounter a love that is greater than fear.

5. How does this change the view of you?

Does your fear kill you or build you up? Negative fear results in despair, but you are challenged by positive fear to resolve it by gaining more confidence. Reasonable fear, the feeling of reverence that comes from wonder, inspires you to learn how strong God is and how much he can encourage you because he loves you in any circumstance you are faced with.

Go ahead and enjoy the thrill of being terrified. Just do this for the right reason: in your life, experience more wonderful. If you open up to think, you can't predict what's going to happen. But when you do, you will feel something greater than yourself. That's sure to be exciting!

1.3 The Benefits of Fear

It's not always a bad thing to fear. It can push us to excellence sometimes. Fear is a human emotion that is tricky. You may be paralyzed. It can deter you from dreaming. It can keep you low. It can keep you safe, as well.

Fear in the right doses can be your companion, but too much can kill you.

Fear tells us that we are at risk. But it's often imagined, it doesn't place the hint. Often, we think things will be hard and then we'll be pleasantly surprised if they don't.

For example, the pressure is a subjective thing. Unless we're thinking about physical strain, our feelings about what's going on usually cause tension. The sense of pressure does not come from the actual event itself. That's what our reasoning behind it is.

Stress is based on fear. We're worried that things won't turn out; that what's going on isn't right somehow. So, we're doing something or not. We are either more tense, or we go into a full release depending on how we react to events, allowing things to happen as they might.

Releasing takes off the stress, allowing anxiety to go home and taking root in even the most challenging situations.

Love the fear of you. That's everything it wants. It only develops when you allow it to overtake you, and typically when we forget how helpful our fear is trying to be. It wants our best, but sometimes it is unreasonable.

Fear can actually be a perfect thing. With moderation, it has its position!

1.4 The Psychology behind Fear

Fear is a human emotion that is strong and primal. It alerts us about the presence of danger, and to keep our ancestors alive, it was critical. Two responses can divide fear: biochemical and emotional. The biochemical response is universal, though highly individual emotional reaction.

Biochemical Reaction:

Fear is a natural emotion and a tool for survival. Our bodies respond in specific ways when faced with a perceived threat. Physical reactions to fear include sweating, high heart rate, and high levels of adrenaline, which makes us very alert.

It is known as the "fight or flight" response is this physical reaction, in which the body prepares to either go into battle or run away. This biochemical reaction is likely to be evolutionary. It's a vital automatic response for our survival.

Response to emotion:

Highly personalized is an emotional response to fear because fear involves some of the same chemical reactions in our brains that positive emotions, such as happiness and excitement, can be seen as fun to feel fear under certain circumstances, such as watching scary films.

Some people are junkies of adrenaline who depend on extreme sports and other circumstances of thrill that cause fear. Others have an adverse reaction to the sense of fear, avoiding situations that induce fear at all costs. While the physical response is the same, depending on the person, fear can be viewed as either positive or negative.

Causes of Anxiety:

Fear is amazingly complex. Many fears may arise from events or trauma, while others may reflect a total fear of something else, such as a loss of control. However, other fears can occur because they cause physical symptoms, such as height fear because they make you feel dizzy and sick.

Acclimatization:

Repeated exposure to similar situations results in familiarity. It dramatically reduces both the reaction of fear and the resulting delight, resulting in adrenaline junkies looking for new and bigger thrills. It is also the basis for specific phobia therapies, which rely on gradually reducing the response of fear by making it feel familiar.

Phobias Psychology:

One component of anxiety disorders may be a propensity to develop fear. Where people tend to experience fear only in situations that are viewed as scary or dangerous, those suffering from anxiety disorders may be afraid they may encounter a fear response. We view their reactions to fear as negative and go out of their way to avoid those reactions.

A phobia is a twist of the normal response of fear. The fear is directed at an entity or circumstance that is not a real danger. Although you understand the fear is irrational, the reaction cannot be stopped. The fear continues to worsen over time as fear of reaction to fear takes root.

Phobias diagnosis:

Phobia therapies based on fear therapy tend to focus on strategies such as systematic desensitization and flooding. Both techniques work to reduce fear with the physiological and psychological responses of your body.

Systematic desensitization:

You are gradually led through a series of situations of exposure in this treatment. For example, you could spend the first session thinking about snakes if you're afraid of snakes. Slowly, during subsequent sessions, you'd be driven by looking at snakes' pictures, playing with toy snakes, and finally handling a live snake. Typically, this is followed by studying and applying new methods of coping to control the reaction of fear.

Flooding:

This is a kind of technique of exposure that can be quite successful. It is based on the assumption that your phobia is a learned behaviour and that you have to unlearn this. During flooding, you are exposed to a vast quantity of the feared object or exposed to a feared condition in a secure, controlled environment for a prolonged period of time until the fear is through. For example, if you're afraid of aircraft, you'd still go up in one. The goal is to get you through the intense anxiety and imminent panic to a position where you face the fear and eventually realize you're OK. This can help to strengthen a positive reaction (you are not in danger) with a feared event (being on a plane in the sky) that ultimately leads you past the fear.

It is necessary to pursue these confrontational methods only with guidance from a qualified mental health professional, as these are potentially traumatic strategies. We have an outstanding rate of success in some cases, however, if you're up to try them.

Chapter 2: Categories of fear common in every person

Nothing can stop you from your full power and to achieve your goals like fear. Fear will hinder your ambition, stall your growth, and keep so far from achieving all your talents, hopes, and dreams that you will eventually take them to the grave. It may be enough to strike you from all sorts of angles and leave you wholly paralyzed, whether it's the fear of public speaking, the fear of going after something you want, the fear of making a fool of yourself, or something else you're afraid of. Many of us are walking around with fear as our destiny's main driver! It can control at any given time every thought, action, and belief you have.

The good news is you don't have to give in to fear and encourage your life to escape. But you need to consider what it is to conquer it, where it comes from and what it means to face it. Read and learn about the various types of fears that exist in our lives and how they can never hold you back.

Phobias are one of America's most common mental disorders. The National Institute of Mental Health seculars that there is some form of phobia in eight percent of U.S. adults. Women develop more phobias than men. Typical phobias signs may include vomiting, tremor, rapid heartbeat, feelings of unreality, and apprehension about the object of fear.

The American Psychiatric Association recognizes three distinct phobias categories: interpersonal phobias, agoraphobia, and phobias. If people talk about having a phobia of a particular object like rats, spiders or needles, they refer to a specific phobia.

Phobias can have a severe impact on well-being, but note that you're not alone. Phobias are common, but can also be treated. When you think you have the signs of some kind of phobia, consult your doctor for further diagnosis and guidance on treatment.

2.1 Fear of People

Anthrop phobia is a social phobia that is often acute and often affects adolescents. By its moral and philosophical side, which is not a phobia, it is distinguished from misanthropy.

What is a condition with social anxiety or social phobia?

Occasionally, many people become nervous or self-conscious, such as giving a speech or interviewing for a new job. But disorder of social anxiety, or social phobia, is more than mere shyness or occasional nerves. Social anxiety

Disorder includes intense fear of certain social situations, especially unfamiliar circumstances in which you believe others are going to watch or judge you. Such scenarios can be so frightening that you just worry about them or go to great lengths to avoid them and ruin your life in the process.

The root symptom of social anxiety is the fear of public scrutiny, criticism, or humiliation. You may be afraid people are going to think badly about you or you're not going to measure up against others. And while you probably realize that at least your fears of being judged are somewhat unfounded even overblown, you can't help feeling nervous. But no matter how shy you may be, and no matter how bad the butterflies may be, in social situations you will learn to be confident and regain your life.

What causes anxiety in society?

Although it may seem that you are the only one with this problem, social anxiety is quite normal in fact. Most people are fighting these fears. But there may be different situations that cause the social anxiety disorder symptoms.

In most social situations, some people experience anxiety. Anxiety is linked to specific social situations for others, such as talking with strangers, mingling at events, or appearing before an audience. Common social anxiety triggers include:

- Meeting new people
- Small speaking
- Public speaking
- Performing on stage

- Being at the center of attention
- Being watched while doing something
- Being teased or criticized
- Talking to "important" people or figures of authority
- Being called in class
- Going on a date
- Speaking at a meeting
- Using public toilets
- Examining
- Eating or drinking in public.

Symptoms of social anxiety disorder

Just because you get confuse in social situations from time to time doesn't mean you're having social anxiety disorder or social phobia. Most people often feel shy or self-conscious, yet it does not interfere with their day-to-day working. On the other hand, social anxiety disorder interferes with your regular routine, causing great distress.

It's perfectly normal, for example, to get the jitters before you give a speech. But if you have social anxiety, you can worry about getting out of it for weeks ahead of time, call in sick, or start shaking so badly during your speech that you can hardly talk.

Emotional symptoms and signs of social anxiety disorder:

- Excessive self-awareness and anxiety in daily social situations
- severe worry for days, weeks or even months before an upcoming social situation

- Healthy fear of being observed or judged by others, especially people you don't know

- Fear that you will act in ways that embarrass or humiliate yourself

- The anxiety that others won't be watched or judged by others.

Physical signs and symptoms:

- Red face or blushing

- Shortness of breath

- Stomach upset, nausea (i.e. butterflies)

- Trembling or shaking (including shaky voice)

- Racing heart or chest tightness

- Sweating or hot flashing

- Feeling dizzy or weak.

Behavioral signs and symptoms:

- Avoiding social situations to the degree that limits your activity or disrupts your life

- Staying quiet or hiding in the back to escape notice and embarrassment

- A need to always bring a buddy with you wherever you go

- Drinking before social situations.

Social anxiety disorder in children

There is nothing unusual about a child being shy, but children with social anxiety disorder experience extreme discomfort over everyday situations such as playing with other children, reading in school, speaking to adults, or taking tests. Kids with social phobia sometimes don't even want to go to work.

How to conquer the syndrome of social anxiety?

Tip 1: Negative thinking challenge.

While there may seem to be nothing you can do about the symptoms of social anxiety disorder or social phobia, there are many things that can actually help. The first step is to test the mind.

Patients with social anxiety have negative thoughts and beliefs that lead to their distress and fears.

- You know you're going to end up looking like a fool.
- Your voice is going to start shaking and you're going to humiliate yourself.

People are going to think you're stupid.
You're not going to have to say something.

Challenging these negative thoughts is an important way of reducing social anxiety symptoms.

Step1: Identify the negative unconscious thinking underlying the distrust of social situations.
For example, if you're stressed about an upcoming presentation of the work, the underlying negative thought might be: you're going to blow it. Everyone will think that you are totally incompetent.

Step 2: Analyze these thoughts and challenge them.

This helps ask yourself questions about the negative thoughts: "Will you know for certain that you will ruin the presentation?" And" Even though you're anxious, do people think you're incompetent?" You can replace them with realistic and positive ways of looking at social situations that trigger your anxiety through this logical evaluation of your negative thoughts.

Thinking about why you feel and think the way you do can be incredibly frightening, but understanding the reasons for your anxieties can help reduce their negative impact on your life.

Unhelpful thinking styles that fuel social anxiety:

Ask yourself if you engage in any of the following unhelpful thinking styles:
• Mind reading: Presuming you know what other people think and see you in the same negative way you see yourself.
• Telling fortune: predicting the future, usually on the basis of the worst. You just "know" things are going to go horribly, so you're already anxious, even before you're in the situation.
• Disastrous: things are blowing out of proportion. For instance, if people notice you're nervous, it's going to be "awful," "terrible," or "disastrous."
• Customizing: Assuming people focus on you in a negative way or what's going on with other people has to do with you.
Tip 2: Focus on others, not yourself.
All of us get caught up in our anxious thoughts and feelings when we're in a social situation that makes us nervous. You may be convinced that you are being looked at and judged by everyone. The concentration is on the body sensations, so you will be able to control them better by paying extra attention. But this intense fixation on yourself makes you more aware of how anxious you are, causing even more anxiety! It also prevents you from reflecting entirely on the interactions that surround you or the quality that you offer.

Moving from an internal emphasis to an external one can go a long way in increasing social anxiety. That's easy to say than to be done, but at the same time you can't pay attention to two things. The more you focus on what's going on around you, the less depression can affect you.

Depend on other people, but not on what they think of you! Instead, do your best to get them involved and make a real connection.

Remember that you don't see anxiety as you think. And even if someone thinks you're anxious, it doesn't mean they're going to think badly about you. Others are likely to feel as anxious as you or have done in the past.

Always listen to what your negative feelings are not being told.

Instead of thinking about what you're going to say or beating up for a flub that's already gone, concentrate on the present moment.

To be fine, release the pressure. Reflect instead on being sincere and attentive qualities that will be respected by others.

Tip 3: Learn how to control your breathing.

When you become anxious, many changes happen in your body. One of the first improvements is that you start breathing quickly.

Over-breathing (hyperventilation) throws off your body's oxygen and carbon dioxide balance leading to more physical anxiety symptoms such as dizziness, smothering, increased heart rate, and muscle tension.

Understanding to slow down your breathing will help restore control of your physical anxiety symptoms.

Practicing the following exercise in relaxation will help you stay calm:

Sit comfortably straight with your back and relax your shoulders. Place your neck with one hand and your belly with the other.

Inhale through your nose deeply and slowly for 4 seconds. The hand on your abdomen will rise, while very little should be pushed by the hand on your neck.

For 2 seconds, hold the breath.

Exhale slowly for 6 seconds through your mouth, blowing out as much air as possible. The hand on your stomach is supposed to move in as you exhale, but very little should move your other hand.

How to Make Fear your Ally

Continue to breathe in and out through your nose. Focus on maintaining a 4-in, 2-hold, and 6-out slow and steady breathing pattern.

Tip 4: Face your fears

The most useful thing you can do to overcome social anxiety is to face, rather than avoid, the social situations you fear. Avoidance keeps the condition of social anxiety running.

Although avoiding nerve-wracking situations can help you feel better in the short term, it prevents you from becoming more confident in social situations and learning how to deal with them in the long run.

Indeed, the more you avoid a feared social situation, the more it becomes frightening.

You may also be discouraged from doing things you would like to do or reaching other goals. For example, you may be discouraged from sharing your ideas at work, standing out in the classroom, or making new friends.

Although a feared social situation may seem difficult to solve, you can do it by taking it one small step at a time.

The trick is to start with a situation you can handle and slowly work your way up to more challenging conditions, building your confidence and coping skills as you move up the "anxiety ladder." For example, if you're nervous about socializing with strangers, you could begin by accompanying an outgoing friend to a party. You may try to introduce yourself to a new person once you're comfortable with that move, and so on.

To work your way up to a ladder of social anxiety: don't necessarily try to face your greatest fear. Moving too fast or forcing things is never a good idea. It may exacerbate your fear and backfire.

Be polite, be careful. It takes time and practice to conquer social anxiety. It is a step-by-step incremental development.

Use your abilities to stay calm, such as concentrating on your breathing and questioning pessimistic theories.

Tip 5: Make efforts to be more social

Another effective way to challenge your fears and overcome social anxiety is to seek supporting social environments actively. Good ways to interact with others in positive ways are the following suggestions: take a class of social skills or assertiveness training. In local adult education centers or community colleges, these classes are often offered.

Volunteer doing something you enjoy, like walking dogs in a shelter or stuffing envelopes for a project that will give you an event to concentrate on while you interact with a small number of like-minded people as well.

Focus on the qualities of your contact. Good relationships rely on clear communication, which is emotionally intelligent. Learning the necessary skills of emotional intelligence can help if you find that you have trouble connecting with others.

Tips to make friends even if you're shy or socially awkward

No matter how uncomfortable or anxious you feel in other people's company, you should learn to suppress self-critical thoughts, raise your self-esteem, and become more confident and secure in your interactions with others.

There's no need to change your personality. You will conquer your fears and anxieties by actually learning new skills and embracing a different outlook and creating rewarding relationships.

Tip 6: Adopt an anti-anxiety lifestyle

Mind and body are inherently linked, and evidence suggests that how you treat your body can have a clear effect on your anxiety levels, your ability to manage symptoms of anxiety, and your overall self-confidence.

While changes in lifestyle alone are not sufficient to overcome social phobia or syndrome of social anxiety, they will help your overall progress in care. The following tips on lifestyle will help you reduce the whole level of anxiety and set the stage for successful treatment.

Avoid or limit the amount of caffeine.

Coffee, tea, soda, and energy drinks alleviate the symptoms of anxiety. Try completely cutting out caffeine, or keeping your consumption low and morning-limited.

Get active.

Make physical activity a priority, if necessary, 30 minutes a day. When you dislike exercising, try to combine it with something you love, like shopping in the window while walking around the mall or dancing to your favorite music.

Fill your diet with more omega-3 fats.

Omega-3 fatty acids support the health of your brain and can improve your mood, outlook, and anxiety management. Fatty fish (salmon, herring, mackerel, anchovy, and sardines), seaweed, flaxseed, and walnuts are the best sources.

Only drink in moderation.

Before a social situation, you may be tempted to drink to calm your nerves, but alcohol increases the risk of an anxiety attack.

Stop smoking.

Nicotine is a potent stimulant. Smoking leads to higher levels of anxiety, not lower, contrary to popular belief.

Get enough sleep of value

You're more vulnerable to depression when you're deprived of sleep. In social situations, being well-rested will help you stay calm.

Treatment of social anxiety disorder

If you have tried the methods of self-help above and still struggle with crippling social anxiety, you may also need professional assistance.

Socio-anxiety therapy

Cognitive-behavioral therapy (CBT) has shown their best for the treatment of social anxiety disorder of all available professional treatments. CBT is based on the logic that what you think affects how you feel and on your actions. So, if you change the way of your thinking about anxiety-giving social situations, you'll feel better and work better.

CBT may include social phobia:

Learning how to manage anxiety's physical symptoms through relaxation techniques and breathing exercises.

It is challenging negative and unhelpful thoughts that cause social anxiety and intensify it, replacing them with more positive views.

In the face of social situations, instead of resisting them, you fear in a gradual, systematic way.

While you can practice these exercises on your own, you may benefit from the extra support and guidance provided by a therapist if you have had trouble with self-help.

Role-playing, instruction in social skills, and other CBT strategies are often as part of a group of counselors. Group therapy includes acting, videotaping and listening, insulting interviews, and other techniques to work on real-world situations that make you nervous. You will become more and more comfortable as you practice and prepare for situations that you are afraid of, and your anxiety will diminish.

Therapy for social anxiety disorder Medicine is sometimes used to alleviate social anxiety symptoms, but it is not a cure. By contrast to counseling and self-help approaches that address the root cause of your social anxiety disorder, medicine is deemed most beneficial.

In the treatment of social anxiety, three types of medication are used:

Beta-blockers are used to relieve anxiety about performance. Although they do not affect the anxiety's emotional symptoms, they may regulate physical symptoms such as shaking hands or speech, sweating, and fast heartbeat.

Antidepressants can be useful in severe and debilitating social anxiety disorder.

Benzodiazepines are anti-anxiety medications that act quickly. These are sedative and addictive, however, so they are generally only used when other medications have not performed.

2.2 Fear of failure

Phobias are irrational fears associated with particular objects or circumstances. You have an irregular and persistent fear of failure if you experience atychiphobia.
Fear of failure can be part of another mood disorder, the disorder of anxiety, or an eating disorder. At times throughout your life, you may also be dealing with atychiphobia if you are a perfectionist.

Symptoms:

This form of fear will not be felt by everyone the same way. The frequency ranges from moderate to severe along a continuum. Phobias such as atychiphobia can be so severe that they can paralyze you entirely, making it difficult to carry out your home, school, or work activities. You may even miss out on significant personal and professional opportunities in your life.

The other atychiphobia symptoms you might encounter are similar to those you would experience with other phobias. In nature, they may be physical or emotional, and most likely; they will be triggered when we think about certain situations where you may fail. In some cases, it may seem that your symptoms come from nowhere at all.

Physical symptoms may include:

- breathing difficulties
- unusually fast heart rate
- tightness or chest pain
- trembling or shaking feelings
- dizziness or lightheadedness
- stomach discomfort
- hot or cold flashes
- sweating

That means you're so scared of failing that you're sabotaging your efforts. You may not start a large school project as an example, ultimately failing as a result. The idea here is that it is better to fail after a lot of effort not to start than to fail.

Emotional symptoms may include:

- extreme feeling of panic or anxiety
- the overwhelming need to avoid a circumstance that causes fear
- feeling disconnected from yourself
- feeling like you have lost control over a situation
- worrying that you may die or pass away
- generally feeling helpless over your fear

Self-handicap is another possibility when you have an atychiphobia. This means you're so afraid of failing that you're sabotaging your efforts. You may not begin a large school project as an example, potentially failing as a result.

The principle here is that it is better to fail after a lot of effort not to begin than to fail.

Risk factors

The exact reason you're feeling a fear of failure can be difficult to identify. The development of phobias includes increasing risk factors. Generally speaking, you may be more likely to develop atychiphobia if:
· You have past experiences where you have failed, particularly if the experiences are stressful or had significant consequences, such as losing out on an important job.
You have learned to be afraid of failing in different situations
You are a perfectionist.
This condition is called an "observational learning experience." For example, if you have grown up with a caregiver who was afraid of failure, it may make you feel the same more likely.
After reading or hearing about the experience of someone else, you may even develop fear. This is called "informative learning." Because of their genes, certain people may be more vulnerable to fear. Not much is understood about fear-related genetics, but in response to feared stimuli, various biological changes may occur in the brain and body.
Specific phobias can affect children and adults alike. While atychiphobia is possible for children, irrational fears at a young age typically revolve around things such as strangers, loud noises, monsters, and darkness. Children between the age of 7 and 16 have more fears based on reality and are likely to experience the fear of failure related to things like performance at school.

Diagnosis

You may have atychiphobia if your fear of failure is severe enough that it has started to affect your daily life. A physician can assist in diagnosing this phobia and recommend treatments to help.

Your doctor can ask you questions at your appointment about the symptoms you experience. Before using different tests to make a formal diagnosis, they may also inquire about your psychological and social history.

You must have symptoms for six months or more to be diagnosed with a phobia.

Other requirements include:

- Extreme anticipation of situations that cause fear
- Immediate response to fear or panic attack in situations that cause fear
- Self-recognition that fear is serious and unreasonable
- Avoidance of situations and items that can cause anxiety.

Treatment:

Treatment of phobias like atychiphobia is individual to each person. In general, main goal of treatment is to improve your quality of life. If you have many phobias, your doctor will treat them one at a time.

Options of treatment may include one or a combination of the following:

Psychotherapy

Your physician may refer you for psychotherapy to a mental health professional. Exposure therapy requires a gradual yet regular introduction to the things you are afraid of in hopes of changing your reaction to them. Cognitive behavioral therapy (CBT) provides communication and other tools to help control the fear of failure. One of these treatments or a combination may be prescribed by your doctor.

Medication psychotherapy in itself is not successful, but medications can help. Medicines are commonly used as a short-term solution for specific situations of anxiety and panic. This can mean taking medicine before public speaking or a big meeting with atychiphobia. Beta blockers: are medications use to block adrenaline from raising your heart rate, increasing blood pressure, and shaking your body. In order to relax, sedatives reduce anxiety.

Changes in lifestyle learning different exercises in mindfulness can help you deal with your fear of failure related anxiety or avoidance. Relaxation techniques can also be successful, such as deep breathing or yoga. Regular exercise is also a good long-term way to manage your anxiety.

2.3 Fear of life

Most people in our society are afraid and run the show in our lives, taking the wheel in most of our decisions. But the thing is, most people don't even know it. It's partially because we prefer to dress up "fear" in the more socially acceptable "stress" clothes in our society. And tension... well, well, stress is almost a sign of success in our culture!

We were taught to think fear is for sissies. We see it as a weakness, something in the dark nights of the soul that we should hide from others and deal with it alone. Yet fear is not supposed to cause guilt or remain hidden. Now our fears need to take centre stage shamelessly so that we can let fear illuminate all that in our lives needs healing and finally be free.

1. You find yourself searching in vain for a standard of perfection that cannot be accomplished
You're going to kill yourself trying to be perfect when you're afraid of criticism, failure, and rejection. The mask of perfection, of course, also separates you from what you want

most: real intimacy, being known, loved, and accepted for your true self.

2. You're settling down

When you're afraid to take risks and step forward for what you want, you're persuaded that Mother Gaya's dismal state is as good as it gets your less-than-juicy life, your relationships, and your work. You forget how to dream when fear runs the show. You compromise in being "realistic," but it's not realism to settle down; it's a crippling sign of anxiety that what you expect is not feasible.

3. When you mean no, you say yes

You'll slip into fear-based, people-pleasing, self-sacrificing habits that lead to disappointment when you're afraid of disappointing people or being rejected if you don't say yes. But when fear no longer runs the show, when it feels self-loving, you say no. Like they say, "No" is a complete expression. It doesn't mean you're not going to devote yourself to service and kindness. It means that the service comes from a sincere motivation based on love (rather than a motivation based on fear).

4. You're saying no if you're saying yes

You're unlikely to take chances if you're afraid. You'll feel like starting your own business, going out with your dream girl, taking that bucket list ride, having a baby, or making an art class. But you're going to say no because you're scared of failing, scared of succeeding, scared of being rejected, scared of stirring up issues, scared of getting out of your comfort zone. You will begin to make your soul take the lead when you let fear heal you, taking straps of faith and saying yes when you yearn for it.

5. You become addicted to alcohol, narcotics, television, or prolonged occupancy

Fear causes inner pain, a sickness of the soul that can appear as depression, anxiety, restlessness, impotence, hopelessness, frustration, sadness, loneliness, and fatigue. You engage in addictions and other addictive behaviours to avoid this inner pain. It only puts a temporary band-aid on the pain, while it increases feelings of low self-esteem which only increases the pain inside.

You will no longer need alcohol, cigarettes, overeating, work holism, painkillers, or other numbing distractions if you are not afraid to be alone with yourself, confront your inner demons, recover from the heart. You will have the confidence to do the transformative research on the other side of your path that will take you to freedom.

6. You procrastinate

In fear of failure, performance, confusion, decision, criticism, or rejection, you will continue to stand on the sidelines where you feel safer. Motivation replaces procrastination when you face head-on terror. You are not "going for it" based on a need to "make it happen" based on fear. Rather, the natural inclination toward love and service produces motivated behaviour that drives you toward that which through you desires to be born.

7. You paralyse yourself

You stop making the decisions that your conscience knows you have to make when you're afraid. Your intuition tells you that this toxic relationship is time to leave. And stop the soul-sucking job. And set your mom's limits. Or go to recovery.

And think about the violations of credibility at work. But the confusion is troubling you.

However, what you will find on the other side of fear is that the key to hope is confusion. Anything could happen if you don't know what the future holds.

8. You're becoming a freak of science

You feel the need to micromanage something when you're afraid. You wrongly think you're living in a violent, random universe that's out to get you away from taking the wheel with both hands and steering your life towards what you want. You don't trust that it's a purposeful world that life is good, that all that happens will help you grow your spirit, even if it's not what your ego wants.

You believe that it is a nice world as you make the journey from fear to faith. You can then relax. Give up on the flow of life, accept what's, let go of the handle, and enjoy the thrilling journey. That's when it's really fun for life.

9. You're muddling yourself

You're going to avoid speaking up while anxiety works on you. You're not going to stand up for what you say. If your dignity is challenged, you will not allow your voice to be heard. If they hurt your feelings, you won't tell anyone. You're going to be too scared to ask what you want.

When you let love lead, the divine voice that flows through you starts to be valued and cherished and you allow it to be heard. As a result, you are going to attract those who resonate with your reality. You're going to find your culture of spirit.

10. That's right. You're getting sick

Fear is not merely an uncomfortable emotion that keeps you from following your dreams. It also causes stress responses in the body that put you at risk for infection and makes it difficult for the body to recover itself. Fearful people are more likely to suffer heart attacks, cancer, diabetes, autoimmune diseases, inflammatory disorders, chronic pain, and even cold. These are also more likely to have milder symptoms such as insomnia, low energy, hypertension, dizziness, headaches, backaches, reduced libido, and gastrointestinal distress.

Not to be afraid!

It's not meant to scare you. It is intended to wake you up, give you hope, and encourage you to embark on the journey from fear to freedom of transformation.

So how are you going to heal fear?

First of all, it's not about curing the fear that can be your partner! It's more about helping you to heal fear. If you develop the right relationship with fear and uncertainty, anxiety may be the finger pointing to everything in your life that needs to be repaired. Here are some things you can do now.

1. Depend on what you love

If you open your heart and encourage yourself to feel gratitude, love will transmute fear almost instantly. Close your eyes and think of a child that you love or a loved one that reaches your heart. Remember the time when you felt wrapped in the arms of Divine Love, when you were struck by a synchronicity, a conception, or a miracle and you realized that you were cherished and protected by a loving heaven. Let the memory of love and connection meets you. Look at the moment when fear dissolves.

2. Its meditating

Meditation is a well-studied and scientifically proven way of reducing anxiety, enhancing your health, ramping up your courage and adapting to the strength of the magic of real life. Try downloading the free "Prescription for Courage" kit if you've never meditated before. It contains guided meditations to relax your nervous system, strengthen your confidence, rewire your fear-based mentality, and help you turn your fear into awakening power.

3. Question your convictions

Question it every time you have a frightening thought. What's true of the thought? What's wrong with this thought? The minute you doubt your thoughts and beliefs, you start distancing yourself, enabling you to take a position of witness to your thoughts. It immediately begins to loosen the grip of terror on you.

4. Confide in the World

Einstein said, the important decision we make is whether we consider that we are living in a friendly or hostile world. Life is scary when you think it's a hostile universe. But you can relax if you trust to be kept, cherished, secure, nurtured, and secured by a guiding intellect.

Whether you ascribe to any particular religion or just call yourself spiritual but not religious, anything that encourages your trust in a welcoming world will allow you to let go and surrender, making your needs and concerns an invitation to the Divine in whatever way you feel authentic.

5. Find the family of the spirit

Having this kind of radical transformation alone is very difficult! Consider another brave spiritually inclined people who make courageous decisions to be their most authentic selves. So, limit your exposure to people (without judging them) who let fear run their lives.

You're going to feel scared and mad if you make this trip alone. But when you look magic that starts to happen when other people live their lives like this, it will inspire you to stay the course even if the journey is difficult. You're just going to have a lot of fun letting your freak flag fly when others float with you.

The Fear of Happiness

Because we are all longing to be happy, we might assume that embracing the prospect of happiness in lives would be an uncomplicated, serene, and automatic operation. But for many of us, however technically attached, we may be to the notion of being happy. It may cause deep ambivalence and fear. We often seem to tend to be stressed and depressed rather than attempting to take on the risks that are secretly related to optimistic moods in our minds. Nevertheless, we can find it paradoxical to be afraid to be happy.

Our anxiety has a past that starts in childhood, where one of the above may have happened. Anyone we loved deeply, and maybe also admired, were sad. Our sorrow moved us profoundly and led us to connect with them to continue to act as a hidden tribute to them as our warning about contentment. Being happy would mean being disloyal in a way that would significantly hurt us. The critical part of us wants to live with them under the canopy of sorrow; however, much they might have inspired us to step out and seize opportunities for joy on the surface. So, without realizing we're doing this, we're making sure we're all going to have a respectable life because they've never had educational opportunities, or because they've been sexually exploited, we turn down sexual opportunities. Instead, someone we were close to might have been jealous of us, causing us to want to downplay our successes and cover our joy–to feel safe from their jealousy and anger. We have learned to mix doom with protection and danger joy. More broadly, any realistic role models for happiness may have been missing. We may have grown up in such an environment in which the default state was being nervous and panicky, where it seemed reasonable to imagine the plane crashing, the police emerging, the company failing, and the mole being cancer. We may be scientifically aware of other ways of viewing the future, but it doesn't sound like what our tribe is doing. We might have included a layer of intellectual superiority to this resistance: joy seems to be misery for the little ones, the leading symptom of rational understanding of the world.

All of these positions lead to a psyche where the advent of joy triggers a severe and conspicuous warning. When we're actually on holiday or in love or surrounded by friends or free from financial pressure, we're panicking. The senses have been stuck in panic mode for so long; when the alarm starts screaming, they are filled with dread.

We are routinely responsible for sabotaging the conditions of contentment to return to a more balanced state. We start working on vacation and soon find a cause for concern in the office; we can complain within hours that we need to go home. Or else we do our utmost to convince a new lover by rarely calling them or (if they don't get the message) having an affair that we're not worth it. To be abandoned, it feels so much more reasonable.

2.4 Fear to lose

Let us assume that we know what we want to leave a relationship, but that we suffer from a problem that prevents us from acting in accordance with our wishes: we cannot bear to cause pain to another person, particularly to another person to whom we feel a sense of loyalty, who has been kind to us, who looks up to us for their protection and future, who has expectations of us and with whom we feel loyalty. Maybe we've come close to telling them a dozen times, but at the last moment, we've still pulled back. We're saying we're going to get around' after the holidays, after their birthday party is over, next year, in the morning,' and yet the deadlines are going on and we're still here.

Their pain has to do with the prospect of unleashing an appalling upset: they will burst into tears, there will be sobbing that can last a very long time, there will be wailing, uncontrollable weeping and piles of wet tissue all because of a reality that lurks in their cranium's recesses at the moment. We're going to be responsible for bringing into turmoil a formerly professional and confident person; it's more than we can handle. It sounds odd, but spending the next few decades unfulfilled may be better for us than just enduring five minutes of unbounded anger. There may also be a panic in another part of our brains. We're more afraid of our partner than we know day by day. We threaten a discharge of titanic rage by telling them that it's over. They that scream at us, accuse us of being a charlatan and a shame to lead them on. Violence and danger may exist.

The thoughts have some symmetry. We will tell them and destroy them by doing so. Or we can warn them that they're going to turn around and kill us, kill or be killed. No wonder we're putting the news off. The reasonable adult part of our minds understands that these thoughts of killing and death cannot be real, but it can weigh very little in the way we feel instinctively. Using sensible arguments can be as successful at times as telling a person with vertigo that the balcony is not going to collapse, or a person with depression that there are perfectly good reasons to be content. Much of the mind is not familiar with hard headed thinking. In an old part of us, we literally work with a sense that either endangering their lives or our own, going against the wishes of a famous person.

As always, when trying to account for irrational and infinite fears, childhood is the place to turn to explain the origins of such terror. Maybe we're the children of a frail parent that we loved deeply, and that disappointment would have broken our hearts. They may have suffered from their mental or physical health; another person might have abused them. Perhaps they relied on us to protect them from desperation or explain their entire lives. We may have derived an early impression that if we were not to cause them severe damage, we would have had to conform to their idea of us, that our wishes and needs could have easily pushed them to the edge, that we might have broken their spirit by being more of ourselves. We just loved them too much and, at the same time, felt that they were too weak to ask them to take our reality on board. We can be three years old and have accepted these messages on board without understanding any of this consciously. And as a result, we might have learned to play very quietly, to rein in our boisterousness or mischievousness, our hostility or our intellect, to be exceedingly cheerful and pleasant around the house, to be' no trouble at all' toward a beloved adult who already seemed to have far too much on their plate.

Instead, we may have been around a person who reacted to any frustration caused by another person with extreme anger for our most vulnerable years. How frightening an angry adult may seem to a delicate two-year-old can be hard to appreciate. Another adult might know that this red-faced figure wasn't going to kill anyone, they're just letting rip for a while, and they're going to pick up the pieces of a smashed vase soon enough, but that's not how it can look through the eyes of a child. How should they know that this individual would not just go one step further several times in size and pick up a hammer at the end of their ranting and knock their skull in? How can they be sure that the briefly completely out of control parent who just opened the door wouldn't push them out of the window as well? Child murder may be utterly alien to the enraged adult, but this is not how a delicate child can be hit. In reality, you don't have to kill anyone to come across to an unformed mind as someone who could be dangerous. We might be a little afraid to share any uncomfortable news, no wonder.

Our minds are freighted with fears stemming from things that happened long ago under precise circumstances but still have a strong, subterranean, barely recognized, and immense impact in our lives today. The challenge is to realize that these fears are genuine, but only in a tiny place: our minds, by taking stock of the past. We are not part of the reality of adults. The tragedy that we expect has already happened: we have already witnessed someone who seemed to risk killing themselves if the news became too bad and somebody who looked like they might kill anyone who displeased them. But in another age, these problems are firmly placed. We need to accept a concept that is always unlikely sounding, we are now adults, which means, and our interactions with others are robust. Another adult is very unlikely to fall on us, and if they do, we will take a lot of action. We're going to know how to help them deal directly and indirectly with their grief. It may seem like it's never going to end, but that's the logic of a child, not an adult. In reality, for a few hours, or days or weeks, it won't be delicious, but ultimately, as it happens, they will resolve it. They're going to recover their good humor; one morning, they're going to wake up and see the world is not over, and they know how to go on. Similarly, they're not going to try to pick up the closest axes and cut us into small pieces. We may be angry, we will scream, there may be some harsh words–but again, we are now healthy and secure, we can get away, in fascism, we have the number of police and a lawyer, we can let the fury escape, and like a well-built bridge in a storm, be utterly assured that we can handle anything that will come our way.

We should note a distinction between being kind and looking kind to give us further courage. It may seem like the kind thing to do is never to threaten or upset someone–and therefore never to send unwanted news to a person we've loved. But that is to neglect the more insidious ways we might destroy the life of somebody. Staying with a person because we want to escape a few hours of unpleasantness is no advantage to them if we then go on for the next few decades to be angry, rude, snide, unfaithful, and depressed. If we offer a life-long foot-dragging scene, we don't help someone by saving them a lousy breakup scene.

A surprising amount of the world's suffering comes from people who are too keen to appear suitable, or rather too timid to inflict short-term pain to others. The courageous way to leave is to encourage someone who still loves us to hate us for a while. We shouldn't think they're never going to find anyone else like us: they might believe it now and even tell us that sweetly. But when they finally understand who we are, they won't believe it. Genuine kindness means getting out, yet if the holiday was booked, the apartment was paid for, and the wedding was planned. There's nothing wrong with the decision that someone isn't for us and nothing serious. While we squeamishly or fearfully hesitate to get out of the way, there is something very wrong about ruining large chunks of someone else's life.

2.5 Fear of public speaking

Fear of public speaking is prevalent, with almost 1 in 4 reporters reluctant to deliver ideas and information to an audience. Being a good speaker is a critical skill that can help you advance your career, develop your company, and build strong relationships.

Although fear helps you to defend yourself in risky situations, allowing fear to stand between you and your audience may prevent you from sharing innovative ideas, talking about meaningful work, and providing new solutions to issues that affect many people. In short, it's the failure of all. We all want to be courageous members of the public. We dream of striding confidently on the stage to give a speech or presentation, cracking the ice with the perfect joke, captivating the crowd with compelling stories, answering with ease the most difficult questions, and leaving to cheers and applause.

Generally, however, truth is less than ideal. Our fears sometimes take over, and we believe that we trip on the stairs, forget our lines, draw a blank, or lose the audience. It is easy to interpret these fears as a warning that a sign that we were not meant to be on the stage in the first place is going to go wrong with something.

What are we going to do about it?

The factors that cause public speaking anxiety are also ones that have been studied by studies to help people conquer it. There are several approaches to overcome public speaking anxiety. Many discuss the physiological dimension of fear, some concentrate on cognitive factors, and some focus on behavioral elements that contribute to higher levels of public-speaking fear and anxiety. Based on this study, this is where to begin:

1. Know how to calm down your body

A variety of relaxation techniques can decrease the increased physiological activity that is automatically produced by the body when faced with an event or situation that causes fear. The stimuli that cause fear in the case of public speaking can range from the actual speaking game itself to the mere thought of having to speak in public. Learning to relax while thinking, preparing, or giving an oral presentation reduces the experience of fear and prevents performance interference. Relaxation techniques include learning how to regulate your breathing, lower your heart rate, and lower your muscle tension. When combined with gradual exposure to public speaking, these techniques work best. For example, before you decide to speak, you start applying these strategies first, then as you practice your speech, and finally, when you deliver it. You could also increase the size of activities slowly as you learn how to manage your anxiety by relaxation, beginning with tiny audiences and going up in numbers little by little. You could start with speeches that are easier to prepare for or less intimidating to deliver to learn the techniques of calming, and then continue to use them as you reach situations where the stakes become exponentially higher. Relaxation is a useful technique with results that are fast but not necessarily long-lasting.

2. Challenge your public-speaking convictions

Another way to overcome public speaking anxiety is to question your assumptions about your ability to prepare and deliver an effective and powerful message. Cognitive reframing strategies address the negative self-declarations (I'm not a good speaker; audiences find me annoying) or any unreasonable public-speaking biases (people can see how nervous I'm on stage). Irrational, in this situation, means that the evidence or the understanding does not reflect your views. Cognitive reframing helps you criticize and substitute negative statements and opinions with optimistic, compassionate, and constructive remarks. It is important that these techniques are not intended merely to substitute vapid and meaningless statements for negative thinking. We encourage you to think more critically and pragmatically. Primarily, you train yourself to see public speaking as a non-threatening experience that you can learn how to navigate and see yourself as a confident, progressive speaker.

3. Shift your focus to communication from results

A different approach to a thought means changing your focus from assessment to interest. You teach yourself to see public speaking as a situation in which you share what you think will benefit from with others, rather than thinking of it as a situation in which you will be evaluated and judged. This change in perspective will relieve you of your anxiety about how you will come across and concentrate on how best to get your message across.

4. Planning, planning, preparing

A public-speaking performance is just the culmination of a comprehensive planning and rehearsal process for your presentation. The more you are prepared, less you will look nervous, forget your notes, or lose your train of thought. Think about the number of actors working to produce full scripts to the public. Approaching the audience as actors approach the performance will help you change your attention from worrying to planning, and the more prepared you are, the more focused you are on your message, and the less disturbed you will be by your anxiety. In this Ted talk, Amy and Michael Port (author of Steal the Show) encourage people to see themselves as performers and apply similar techniques in high-stakes situations that involve sharing ideas and information with other people that actors use to "create a reality of their choice." Such an approach enables you to achieve your goal while maintaining authenticity at the same time. Note, it is always more anxious to be under-prepared than to be over-prepared.

5. Seek out more chances of talking

Whether you're working on your body's reactions to anxiety, your opinion of yourself as a speaker, or your general public-speaking style, the more experience you gain, the more trust you gain. Finding and creating opportunities for speaking allows you to practice and build on what you have learned. It also helps you learn how to use your own experiences to improve your presentation skills further. Primarily, instead of punishing yourself for it, you benefit from what didn't work well. And the more you speak, the more you know that what makes a good speaker is a combination of the noble purpose of educating or encouraging an audience, a positive attitude, and a lot of preparatory work.

6. Ask for assistance

You can do a lot to release the fear of talking to the media on your own; there are a lot of opportunities for some extra help. Getting aid can be a more efficient way to achieve outcomes in many situations than doing it alone. Many validated approaches are available to help resolve public speaking issues and many trained practitioners providing them. Besides asking for help from experts, there are consumer-organized groups such as Toastmasters that also offer opportunities to build your skills in a non-threatening and non-committal environment. To directly resolve their fear of public speaking, many people join these groups.

The main line is that if something scares you, you're going to avoid it, and if you prevent it, you're not going to get enough practice. If you don't get enough exercise, you're not going to get better, and if you don't get better, you're going to continue to be afraid of it. The period of fear will remain and continue. But there's no need for it's his is up to you to decide when and how to break this cycle of public-speaking anxiety with the number of options available.

2.6 Fear of height

When we're at a great height, most of us feel a little nervous and anxious. Indeed, feeling this way is perfectly normal and understandable. Nonetheless, a 1960 study showed that even babies and young animals have an inherent fear of falling. If you have acrophobia, however, you may find that even relatively low altitudes cause you to panic. If you are dealing with height anxiety, to the degree that it makes life difficult, don't worry, you can conquer it!

How can you conquer a heights fear?

If you're reading this and dealing with heights, the first thing you're likely going to want to learn is how to conquer it. We will discuss this in-depth in this post, as well as give you more details about the acrophobia itself. But first, a few quick tips are here to help you make progress.

- Take time to prepare yourself mentally

- Visualize yourself to overcome your fear

- Slowly move

- Breathe

- Go easy on yourself.

Whether you have fear of height or a true phobia, you may be uncertain. To help, we have made a list of acrophobia-related symptoms. These include feeling any of the following if you think regarding the possibility of heights or are faced with it.

- A feeling of unreality

- Trying to catch your breath

- Fast breathing

- Increased or rapid heart rate

- Trembling

- Sweating

- Dizziness

- Fear of injury or death

Fear of height avoidance. You may also suffer from height panic attacks; this is particularly dangerous as you may fall and hurt yourself.

Simultaneous Symptoms Occurring In addition to a Fear of Heights, other phobias go hand in hand with acrophobia, unfortunately. Alongside your height anxiety, these can be viewed and include:

Aerophobia. Intense fear of flying or being in the air

Bathmophobia. Intense fear of seeing slopes or stairs.

Climacophobia, Intense fear of falling or ascending from a height

Illyngophobia.

It is very reasonable to have an intense fear of feeling dizzy when at a high height (vertigo) How to treat your fear of heights. Instinctive fear of top places, hence, everybody has some degree of it. Height fear can stop you from entering potentially dangerous or life-threatening situations such as falling off a cliff or stumbling off a bridge. But, if you are dealing with a severe phobia, you may not even be able to go up a ladder for a few steps without becoming very depressed. How can you do it without panicking if you find yourself in a situation that needs you to be at a height? The following steps may be helpful.

Be prepared when you know you need to be in a position where you need to be at a height; take some time to brace yourself mentally.

Visualize Yourself Overcoming Your Anxiety Take a few minutes to close your eyes and see how safe your situation is. Consider using your rational mind to reassure you that you're not going to fall or injure yourself. Enable these thoughts to become one with your subconscious, so you can rely on them to help you stay calm and focused when you begin to feel upset and frightened.

Take Things Slowly Confront your fears at your own pace instead of jumping straight into a worrying situation. Start by setting yourself some small initial objectives, such as standing on a chair or every day moving a little closer to your balcony railing. Only gradually work on this, and success will be yours quicker than you might think at the moment.

When you're nervous, you can forget to breathe correctly. And make sure you get plenty of oxygen into your brain by concentrating on taking deep, daily breaths.

You have a phobia; don't be too harsh on yourself. In a day, phobias can't be resolved. If you've been panicking and running from a challenging situation, don't beat yourself. Be sweet on your own. Perhaps consider seeking a professional's advice.

Having A Fear of Heights Is Common-Here's How to Overcome It Treatments:

For Your Fear of Heights If you've been suffering from symptoms of acrophobia for a while, there are things you can do to start overcoming this paralyzing fear and start living a fulfilled life. Let's look at the possibilities.

Exposure and System Desensitization Therapy, your fear of heights, may gradually become desensitized, although this method may take many months or years to be fully capable. It's hard to be continuously exposed to heights, as you might imagine, so some therapists are using virtual reality to help.

Besides, height-related activities such as ascending a steep flight of stairs can be shared with you. The therapist advises you to slowly increase the height while helping you to reduce the level of fear. The therapist also teaches you practical methods of calming to cope with your anxiety. These may include mental visualization, breathing control, and muscle relaxation; this treatment aspect is intended to help you relax when faced with an anxious situation.

Medicines are commonly used in phobias care. For example, to control your symptoms, your doctor can prescribe antidepressants or anti-anxiety medication.

Cognitive Behavioral Therapy (CBT)

CBT addresses the underlying issues that have contributed to your phobia, unlike anxiety medications. And adequately prepare yourself with the knowledge you need to resolve your phobia, you learn to understand your fears and worries. Two main factors are involved in counseling: • Behavioral therapy. The focus in cognitive therapy is how negative thoughts contribute to your anxiety • Behavioral treatment. Behavioral therapy focuses on how you respond and behave in conditions that cause anxiety. CBT is often useful in height fear care. The treatment focuses on acrophobia-related negative images and thinking. The therapist is working with you to remove constructive adverse reactions. Then you can change your terrifying response, making it a positive one. CBT explores how your emotions influence how you feel and decide how you view each situation.

Complementary therapies

You can also integrate complementary therapies into your life to help you find the balance you need as you discuss the fear of heights with the help of a therapist or in any way you feel is correct for you.

Return to biofeedback.

Biofeedback uses sensors, such as muscle tension, heart rate, and breathing, to monitor certain physiological functions. Then you can know the solutions to your body's fears and learn to control them by relaxation techniques.

Hypnosis

Hypnosis is used to help people cope with their concerns; it can help the person re-evaluate their anxiety and see in a new light the thing that causes their phobia.

The method of relaxation

Relaxation techniques help you feel better when confronting a phobia emotionally. Visualizations, a meditation on consciousness, controlled breathing, and gradual relaxation of the muscle are some of the strategies that can help.

2.7 Fear of death

Thanatophobia is a type of anxiety that is characterized by a fear of one's death or dying cycle. It's commonly referred to as fear about death.

Death anxiety is not described as a distinct condition, but it may be associated with other disorders of depression or anxiety.

These include:

- Post-traumatic stress disorder or PTSD

- Panic disorders and panic attacks

- Diseased anxiety conditions previously referred to as hypochondriasis. Thanatophobia is distinct from necrophobia, which is a general fear of death or death.

Further discuss the signs, triggers, and treatments for this fear; we take a closer look at thanatophobia or death anxiety.

The word' Thanatos' refers to death in the Greek language, and' Photos' means terror. Therefore, thanatophobia is the fear of death.

Death fear is an entirely normal part of the human condition. Nevertheless, thinking about their death or the dying process can cause intense anxiety and fear for some people.

If they find death to be imminent, a person can feel extreme anxiety and fear. You may also experience:

- Afraid of separation

- Afraid of coping with a loss

- Afraid of leaving loved ones behind when these anxieties occur and interfere with everyday life and activities, this is called thanatophobia.

Such feelings can stop people from doing day-to-day tasks or even from leaving their homes in their extreme. Our fears focus on things that might lead to death, such as pollution or toxic products or individuals.

Symptoms and treatment Physicians do not recognize thanatophobia as a distinct condition but may classify it as a specific phobia.

A phobia is an anxiety disorder related to a specific event or situation, according to the Diagnostic and Statistical Manual of Mental Disorders.

- Fear of death is considered as a phobia if anxiety:

- occurs almost any time a person thinks about dying

- Lasts more than six months.

- Gets in the way of everyday life or relationships. Common signs that a person may have a phobia of dying include:

- acute fear or anxiety when thinking about dying or the process of dying

- panic attacks that may cause dizziness, hot flushes, trembling,

The symptoms may come and go through the lifetime of a person. Someone with mild anxiety about death may experience heightened anxiety when they think about their death or a loved one's death, such as when they are seriously ill or a family member.

When death anxiety is associated with another anxiety or depressive disorder, a person may also experience specific symptoms related to the conditions underlying it.

Causes and types of thanatophobia:

Although thanatophobia is characterized as a general fear of death, this anxiety has many forms and causes, and the details of what a person focuses on may differ.

Phobias are often caused in a person's past by a particular event, although the individual doesn't always know what it was. Specific causes for thanatophobia might include a first traumatic event linked to near-death or a loved one's death.

A person suffering from severe disease may experience thanatophobia because they are anxious to die, but ill health is not sufficient for an individual to feel this anxiety. Instead, it is often associated with psychological distress.

Death anxiety experience can vary depending on individual factors. These are:

Age: A study suggests that older adults dread the process of dying, while younger people fear death itself more often.

Gender: Women fear more than men the death of loved ones and the implications of their death, according to a 2012 survey.

Medical professionals correlate fear about death with a variety of mental health conditions, including depressive disorders, PTSD, and anxiety disorders.

Thanatophobia may be associated with: specific phobias Death anxiety is associated with a number of specific phobias. Phobias ' most popular stimuli are things that can cause harm or death, like snakes, spiders, planes, and heights.

Panic disorders in many anxiety disorders, such as panic disorders, fear of dying plays a role. People may feel a loss of control during a panic attack and an intense fear of dying or imminent doom.

Disease anxiety disorders Death anxiety may be associated with disease anxiety disorders, previously referred to as hypochondriasis. Here, an individual is associated with an intense fear of becoming ill and excessive health concerns.

Speaking therapy can aid in the treatment of thanatophobia.

Networks of social support can help protect a person from death anxiety.

Some people may come to terms with death through religious beliefs, although in others, they may maintain a fear of death.

Those with high self-respect, good health, and a belief in living a fulfilling life are less likely to fear death than some others.

A doctor may prescribe medication for an anxiety disorder, phobia, or a particular underlying cause of their fear to a person with thanatophobia.

A type of behavioural or talking therapy is involved in care. This therapy aims to help the patient to recentralize their worries and to work through them by voicing their issues.

Death anxiety treatment options include: cognitive behavioural therapy (CBT) Cognitive behavioural therapy or CBT operates by gradually changing the behavioural patterns of a person to form new attitudes and ways of thinking.

A doctor will assist a person in finding practical solutions to overcome their anxiety feelings. They may work to develop strategies that enable them to be calm and fearless when they talk or think about death.

Psychotherapy, or talk therapy, involves talking to a psychologist or psychotherapist through anxieties and fears. Such practitioners will help someone figure out the cause of their anxiety and come up with strategies to deal with daytime anxieties.

Just thinking about anxiety can sometimes help a person feel more in control of their fear.

Exposure therapy works by helping a patient cope with their fears. Children are encouraged to be open to their worries instead of hiding how children feel about death or not voicing their concerns.

In a safe environment, a therapist can administer exposure therapy by introducing a person to their fear quite slowly until the reaction of anxiety is decreased, and a person can address their thoughts, events, or feelings without fear.

Medication if a person with a severe mental health condition, such as general anxiety disorder (GAD) or PTSD, is diagnosed by physicians, anti-anxiety medication may be prescribed. It may include treatment for beta-blockers or antidepressants.

These are often the most effective when people use drugs alongside psychotherapies.

Although medication can be helpful in the short term by relieving fear and stress feelings, the ideal solution may not be long-term use of such medicines. Alternatively, it is more likely to provide long-term support and function past counselling concerns.

Relaxation strategies it can be essential to practice self-care to boost overall mental health, including making a person feels better able to cope with their anxieties. Many approaches to exercise self-care are to avoid alcohol and caffeine, get a good night's sleep, and follow a nutritious diet.

Specific relaxation techniques can help clear your mind and de-escalate your fears when a person is experiencing anxiety. These may include:

- doing deep breathing exercises
- focusing on particular room objects like counting tiles on the wall

- Meditation or focusing on positive imagery.

Quick information on phobias

Phobias are more severe than mere feelings of fear and are not limited to specific triggers ' fears.

While people are aware that their phobia is irrational, they are unable to control the reaction of fear.

Sweating, chest pain, and pins and needles may be symptoms.

Medication and behavioural therapy may be included in treatment.

In the United States, 19 million people have a phobia.

Chapter 3: What causes fear?

Three factors can differentiate the family of frightening experiences:

Intensity: How serious is the threatened harm?

Timing: the damage is immediate or imminent?

Coping: What, if any, can be done to reduce or remove the threat?

It decreases or eliminates anxiety when we can cope with the danger. Additionally, this intensifies the fear when we are unable to reduce the threat of harm.

A pain potential, or an unrecognizable occurrence, is causing fear. The amygdale, the limbic system's nerves, senses these possibilities and sends out the signals which produce the emotion of fear, which sets off behaviors of avoidance. Unlike the rational brain, several instinctual attitudes and actions cause emotions. The limbic brain selects each such emotion to meet a particularly demanding life contingency. The emotion of frustration changes to behaviors and attitudes that support conflict. On the other hand, fear reacts to danger by remembering threatening memories, preparing the body for flight, and signaling the action of escape, directing the muscles to freeze or fleeing.

Fear is behaving instantly. Before you can walk to the bottom of a precipice, it will stiffen your muscles. Although signals of fear act swiftly to avoid danger, once danger becomes imminent, they escalate. Signs of fear hinder conscious thought in such situations and set off unconscious searches for escape routes while training the body to freeze, flee, or protect it. Such unconscious people are searching for snap pictures of the failure effects. A lack of means of escape intensifies the emotion of terror. Together, the memories that have been recalled, the impulses to run, and the body's pressure preparations sound painful.

- Amygdale-triggered anxiety is one of the earliest survival mechanisms in nature.

- Much fear is a response to the horror of life's painful experiences.

- Anxiety creates a series of biochemical events that consume the mind in the body.

- Most health problems stem from repeated attacks of terror.

- Historically traumatic occurrences, perceptions of pain, and the unknown cause anxiety.

- Panic starts with a shocking reaction.

- Fear in the modern world is simply an obsolete response.

- Most unconscious behavior leads to fear.

- Scientists have found chemicals that might one day mitigate the effects of unnecessary fear.

- The key to dealing with anxiety is self-awareness.

An evolutionary mechanism of survival

Nature developed the amygdale as special-purpose organs in the brain during the early beginnings of life to remember and respond to danger signals. They become sensitive to sensory signals that accompanied painful events in the past. Such tolerance has been thoroughly tested in animal tonsils. A rat is subjected to a sore foot shock in standard experiments accompanied by a vibration.

Earlier, when the noise is heard alone, the tonsil can fire signals of terror. Such unpleasant experiences were seen in the development of "speed dial (LTP) circuits," which responded to the associated sound signal immediately afterward. The organs became more sensitive to these signals. Earlier components of the brains of fish, amphibians, reptiles, birds, and mammals were as crucial as the vertebrae. The amygdale identified hazard patterns as the primary defense response mechanism and allowed animals to combat, freeze, or flee.

Fear and horror

Fear is expressed as fear, anxiety, dread, terror, and panic at increasing levels. The imminence of danger defines these amounts. The prospect of damage in the future causes fear and anxiety. The immediate nature is concerned with fear, terror, and panic. Shock and anxiety overtake people at the highest levels, causing unreasonable decisions to be made. While panic is a fear of imminent danger, horror is a sickening and painful experience. Horror is the emotion that lays the foundation for the tonsil to experience the memories of traumatic incidents. The amygdale remembers the photos, sounds, sentences, and circumstances that followed the trauma of injury, mockery, social rejection, loved one's loss, or career failure. The detection of any related signals subsequently triggers fear, often without the person knowing the cause of their fear.

Responses from the body

The hypothalamus works reflexively to regulate the body's sexual, vegetative, endocrine, hormonal, emotional, and autonomic functions while receiving fear signals from the amygdale. Breathing, digestion, circulation of the blood, brain activity and fluid movements of the body are affected immediately. The amygdale impulses dilate pupils and increase the frequency of brain waves. They're leaving the hair hanging on the edge. They lower the saliva and dry the mouth. They cause sweating and skin resistance to decrease. They are increasing the peripheral flow of blood and trigger cold hands. The signals speed up the respiration and dilate bronchial tubes to allow the lungs to get more oxygen. We contract the muscles of the stomach, delay digestion, and close the excretory process. In the stomach, they increase acids, causing diarrhea.

The stimuli pass to the adrenal gland, which generates cortical, causing an increase in the output of glucose to provide the muscles and brain with additional fuel to cope with the possible stress. The blood pressure is raised by the stimuli, removing cells. We contract muscles of the neck, triggering tremors of the hand and body. To allow higher blood flow, they dilate blood vessels into skeletal muscles. We slow down the immune system's work. The tonsil activates a series of physiological events and engulfs the mind in the emotion of terror even before the conscious mind can evaluate the situation. These pervasive signs of anxiety are not set off by real physical threats in the modern world. These are caused by a mechanical brain that seeks to solve social and job challenges by training the body foolishly to freeze, escape, or protect it.

It has an impact on the long term

A chronic lack of dangerous escape routes leads to insistent panic fear signals that increase heart rate and blood pressure over time. It is suspected that such symptoms lead to heart palpitations, tiredness, vomiting, and chest pain, shortness of breath, stomach aches, or headaches. Escalating signals of anxiety cause panic attacks that have signed similarly to heart attack symptoms. Anxiety has been associated with health issues over the years, including arthritis, migraines, asthma, ulcers of the stomach, and thyroid disease.

Hereditary

The amygdale triggers signals of fear that drive you out of danger. It reacts to three different types of events. The first set of circuits inherited fire to identify historically harmful activities. The second group of neurons grows channels of LTP that learn to fire on the detection of events that followed painful experiences. The last group of channels causes fear when an event's effect cannot be detected by the system.

Triggers from the Past

Nature has built a database of adverse incidents in the amygdale over millions of years. The amygdale automatically reacts to the detection of signs of such events by inducing fear. Therefore, many people have an inherited fear of falling, suffocating in enclosed spaces, drowning in water, and being attacked by rodents, cockroaches, or snakes. Both stage anxiety and public-speaking fear stem from an inherent fear of becoming a target of predator attention. The amygdale's fear responses to such incidents are often accompanied by a shocking reaction.

The experiences of pain

The amygdale provides an extra tolerance to experiences of pain over a lifetime. Anxiety may have arisen from physical injury, traumatic confrontations, loss of loved ones, loss of social standing, or social rejection. Mirror neurons also cause pain in us when we see other people's painful experiences. The amygdale retains memories of the associated sensory sensations whenever such pain has been felt. The flickering picture of an angry face can evoke fear. People are worried about disappointment, about being mocked, about the loss of loved ones. If a person has been traumatized, she may be afraid of loneliness when left alone as a child.

The Unknown

People are afraid of death, nuclear wars, violence, or even forced changes to their work environments without the experience of such incidents. Also, triggering fear is the inability to identify the significance of an event. Archie de Barker writes about the role of confusion in the cause of fear. He tracked stress levels in subjects by calculating pupil diameter changes directly associated with the release of the neither stress hormone nor adrenaline in the brain. He found that pain and discomfort play an approximately equal role in stress.

If they knew they would suffer pain, subjects showed less anxiety than when they did not know if they would avoid the experience of pain. It is useful to list the issues that bother you when fear envelops you for a reason you are unable to fathom. You will find that you will be safe from the emotion by finding the source of such anxiety and addressing it. Even accepting uncertainty as your environment's inevitable facet will reduce your fear as well.

The Startle Answer

Fear begins with the initial response. It is the response (20 milliseconds) of the mind to danger through a direct amygdale fear pathway, as reported by Joseph E. Le Dour. He identified a second route of (300 milliseconds) through the reasoning processes of the cortex, which can proceed to still a sudden onset of fear. Small movements, sounds or images can trigger the fearful startle response. The reflex is arising by birth.

When a new born senses a possibility of falling, her back arched, and her arms and legs flail out. Doctors test the reflex to be sure of an infant's nervous system by simulating a sense of falling by allowing its head to drop slightly. The startle signals from the amygdale activate the sympathetic system, which heightens emotional arousal. Later, the cortical signals may energize the parasympathetic system, dampening down nervous tension. Unsought fear set off by the initial response may be stilled by the reasoned cortical signals, such as when a coiled snake is identified to be just a garden hose.

An Outdated Response

Although the physical danger was ever-present in the primitive world, it is less relevant today. Unfortunately, though warranted by a tiger in the vicinity, fear reactions are unsuitable and unhealthy for a person who is facing career hurdles. The chances of dismissal from work require a calm and arranged reaction. Anxiety causes visions of unpaid bills and sets in your chest, the tightness that does not serve any useful purpose. If you had a solution to the problem, you would know it right away. Out of uncertainty, concern, and depression rarely find solutions. However, they affect your health. Fear is an insignificant animal reaction except to prevent sudden physical injury. The reason of such fear is a primitive neuronal signal from the amygdale that can be stilled by self-awareness training.

Avoidance of sub consciousness

In the moment an animal detects a threat, it determines a course of action–likely sliding under a rock. Fear is a creative process that searches the mind subconsciously for ways to escape pain. You may not be confronted with any conscious awareness of the specific pain you want to stop when your impulsive actions are caused by fear. Some human feelings, including grief, abhorrence, disgust, humiliation, and remorse, and shame, cause pain, etc. Fear of being mocked can cause a person to decide not to participate in the conversation. Fear of feeling the emotion of fear can cause a person to avoid challenging tasks.

References in chemistry

Within the amygdale, fear is triggered as its nerve junctions develop particular sensitivity to specific sensory signals. Only faint noises may cause patients with post-traumatic stress syndrome to undergo intense reactions to fear. Richard Humane discovered that timely modulation of different molecules in the amygdale of animals that control synaptic plasticity can suppress the response of fear. He found an abnormal protein that emerged in animals' amygdale that was trained to respond to sounds that followed a foot shock.

The compound, which only lasted for a few days, seemed to strengthen the amygdale's fear circuits. When the researchers removed the protein during this time, those triggered fearful memories were permanently lost by the animals. Every day, a mix of clinical and pharmacological treatments can be used to help patients with these molecular targets. Zurich scientists also found that the amygdale function was also decreased by the hormone oxytocin related to stress and sex.

Overcoming Anxiety

Self-consciousness can through fear triggers. The extreme activity in the amygdale can be decreased by the brain's attention center–the rostra anterior cingulated cortex (ACC), which triggers the perception of fear. Researchers at Columbia University found that rack worked to dampen amygdale activity when fear signals are viewed consciously. Self-awareness and a few cognitive management exercises will make noticeable, and thus, still its influence the global effect of fear. Conscious awareness and recognition of the perception of fear will tend to be amygdale activity for ordinary people. The practice of self-awareness will offer a relaxed and still mind with the confidence that fearlessness can become an acquired habit.

Creative leadership requires patience, not fear. Fear is paralyzing. Every view seems to be dangerous and threatening. You can do one of three things in any threatening situation. Does something, stop it, or deal with it. A quiet assessment will establish the response and the fear. There will still be knowledge of the threat. Once fear is overcome, common sense emerges. It is the ability to take the calculated risks that make a successful venture.

3.1 Consequences of fear

Worry is our psyche's process that drives us to do something. Fear is the motivating forces typically fears of some consequence. The person tends to avoid talking about it because it's fear. Therefore, worry continues to perpetuate itself circularly– anxiety cause non-action, and failure to act causes more concern.

Anxiety is a fear that has a non-specific or fuzzy element, whereas anxiety is something existent and known. Anxiety is the product of recurring unprocessed thoughts in one's unconscious. It has become a vague feeling about an impending disaster, but because it is undefined, it cannot be dealt with. To solve it, it must first be converted to specific concerns, and then the guidelines on how to deal with worry can be applied.

Panic is an overwhelming fear that confuses the person and makes it unclear what to do. It is the cumulative product of many unresolved and futile doubts, concerns, and anxieties. It sometimes leads to attacks of panic, those unexplained feelings that may not have any immediate cause, but only manifest in the individual.

Phobias are fear-reactions which are

(a) Out of proportion to actual danger, such as jumping and shrieking at a rat or cockroach's vision, or

How to Make Fear your Ally

(B) Irrational, such as trembling when seeing a spider's image.

 Trauma is an emotional "wound," which is a person who can still cause distress. Strictly speaking, with varying degrees of intensity, developed fears are real traumas. But an injury is chronic when it triggers recurrent anxiety-like flashbacks, extreme reactions to anything that reminds one of it or seriously disturbs one's daily life and work.

Envy is a more nuanced emotion, as it is a combination of many things: low self-esteem, anger, and anxiety. They do not resent the accomplishments or contributions of those we can connect with, that is, those we love and care about. Our successes are also our vicariously. On the other hand, the achievements of those we cannot identify with are perceived as threats to our self-esteem, particularly those we dislike.

Feeling puzzled and perplexed at the same time, humiliation requires a "loss of face." The embarrassment may not have been induced by anyone, as if one "disgracefully" slips and falls down. Thus, there is no reason for resentment (except perhaps oneself) towards anyone. The intention is to retreat and run, not to face men. Anxiety about what people might think or say is at its heart. Shame is a feeling close to that.

Consequences of work-related fear:

The consequences of fear depend to some degree in the form of anxiety. But, generally speaking, we need to be attentive not to lie about fear to ourselves.

It's easy to believe that with our feelings, we can be alone that our worries in our gray matter are personal and locked away.

With their thoughts, humans are never alone. Through them, God is always present. God knows that we and everybody else have and will ever have every opinion.

For another cause, too, we are not alone with our fears: our fears guide our behavior.

If we're afraid to trick others, we're going to make decisions to mitigate disappointment.

If we fear change, we're going to make choices that will minimize change.

Often our acts tell a lot about our fears. Fears have consequences because we are acting on our fears and the consequences of our actions.

Consider the consequences of the fear of speaking and the fear of losing power.

The danger of fear, Nelson suggests, is that men prefer not to be "risk-averse" in their economic thinking. It is appropriate for women to base their decisions on fear of negative consequences in this societal context, but men who do so may be perceived as weak or unmanly. As economic markets revolve around the desire of people not to look averse to risk, such demands are more likely to crash and burn, as happened in the late 2000s. If anything, fear of terror worsens hysteria when things eventually go wrong, she writes: "Fear, held unexamined and weakened for too long, may then manifest in abundance when a crisis finally arrives, e.g., in financial panic or in favor of totalitarian means to restore order." How does this affect everyday life? In some situations, fear may be a "logical emotion," but what if not? Are there occasions when your worries blown out of proportion, particularly concerning individuals? If so, who are the people, and why are you afraid of them?

Here are some of the adverse effects of terror:

Fear of authority.

Most people are afraid of their bosses. An employer or boss manages your economic stability. Nevertheless, there are checks in the contemporary workplace against a capricious boss who acts in a moment of anger by dismissing a professional employee. Due process and compliance with union laws protect workers from this, as does the assumption that many managers trust management and superiors working collegially to improve productivity. When they behave in unpredictable and aggressive ways, it is likely that some bosses deserve to be feared. Yet people can also impose their childhood fears of damage or disapproval on employers who are not behaving in nervous ways.

Growing fear

Gender dynamics can also influence the relationships that men and women have in the workplace, according to Nelson's study. Men can create more anxiety for themselves by stifling their fears to avoid looking weak. We don't want to say we fear being killed, causing the undercurrent of anxiety to rot for weeks, months, or years. Because of uncertainty, supervisory assessments may even be prevented, which would help them act as more flexible workers.

The productivity drops

According to this study, women who are trying to look more "competent" (and male-like) can also try to hide their emotional reactions. From the company, these conditions impair the ability of workers to relax and be successful.

The failures of the partnership

Romantic partners and spouses may come to fear the reactions of each other, particularly if the home has a history of uncontrolled rage. Nonetheless, partners can grow more secure over the years in relationships that are not marked by violence and learn to resolve their irrational fears. Even if something goes wrong (when you drop and break another dinner plate), you are no longer afraid of your partner's reaction. The people you are less close to daily are probably more likely to trigger your fears: for example, what will your in-laws do if you don't send a letter of thank-you for a birthday present, or send someone you don't like? In these situations, you may not be afraid of physical harm but rejection.

The Fear of Speaking Up

What are the consequences for you and the organization when fear of speaking up strikes us?

The company doesn't profit from your experience

People won't know that you have knowledge of the subject and won't go to you for advice in the future so the organization won't benefit from your expertise on an ongoing basis.

 You might be viewed as not very concerned or enthusiastic about your job

 If you're speaking up, you may suggest something that isn't important or correct so by no way. You might wonder why people are not listening to you or paying attention to your ideas, and bitterness may be creeping.

The Fear of Losing your Control

It can have the exact opposite effect as being afraid to speak. You may wind up talking too much in your desire to control things. You can "sell" your ideas endlessly to the point that you are not listened to or appreciated by anyone.

By concentrating on your influence rather than the broader picture, you may be perceived to have a personal agenda that does not fit with the goals and objectives of the company

You may be viewed as deceptive, inflexible, pushy, or perhaps territorial.

3.2 What fear does to your mind?

Most of the people don't have to think about having to breathe, digest our food, or make our heartbeat. The autonomic nervous system is responsible for these functions that we consider to be automatic.

It is divided into two branches:

The parasympathetic nervous system (the rest and digestive system), and the sympathetic nervous system (the method of battle or flight).

Fear kicks the reaction to fight or flight into overdrive, says Evans. The adrenal glands secrete adrenaline. Blood flow falls to the frontal lobe of your brain, which is responsible for rational thinking and planning and to take over the deeper, more animalistic parts of your mind, including the amygdale.

Fear on Earth may be as old as life. To protect species from perceived danger to their identity and experience, it is a necessary, profoundly wired reaction developed over the biology past. Fear can be as plain as an antenna sigh in a felt snail, or as complex as a human being's existential anxiety.

If we love fear or hate it, it's hard to deny that we undoubtedly respect it, devoting a whole vacation to the celebration of terror.

Some of the critical chemicals that contribute to the response of "fight or flight" are also engaged in other positive emotional states, such as joy and anticipation, thinking about the circuitry of the brain and human psychology. It makes sense, therefore, that the high anxiety we feel during a scare can also be viewed in a more positive light. But what is the difference between getting a "boost" and feeling terrorized?

They are psychologists who research their neurobiology and treat anxiety. Our researches and clinical interactions, as well as others, suggest that the context has to do with a significant factor in how we experience fear. If our "thinking" brain provides input to our "emotional" brain and we consider ourselves to be in a safe space, then we can quickly shift the way we experience the high excitement, from one of fear to one of joy or excitement.

For example, when you visit a haunted house during the Halloween season, you can easily enjoy the experience by expecting a ghoul jumping out at you and realizing that it's not a threat. In comparison, if you walked through a dark alley at night and a stranger started chasing you, both your brain's emotional and thinking areas will agree that the situation is dangerous, and it's time to flee!

The fear reaction starts in the brain and spreads through the body to make the best defense or flight reaction changes. The response to fear begins in a brain region called the amygdale. This almond-shaped array of nuclei in the brain's temporal lobe is devoted to sensing the stimuli's emotional salience—how much we stand out from everything.

For example, when we see a human face with emotion, the amygdale activates. For anger and fear, this reaction is more pronounced. A risk signal, such as a predator's vision, causes a fear response in the amygdale that stimulates areas involved in combat or flight training for motor functions. It also triggers stress hormones to be released and a sympathetic nervous system.

It leads to changes in the body that allow us to be more active in a hazard: the brain is hyper-alert, the pupils dilate, the bronchi dilate, and the breathing accelerates. There is a rise in heart rate and blood pressure. Increase blood flow and blood flow to the skeletal muscles. Not vital organs like the gastrointestinal system slow down in survival.

Like an animal that attempts to avoid being eaten by a predator, all the resources of your body are diverted to one goal: to remain alive. Increasing your heart rate and blood pressure, breathe faster, and stretch your muscles. The eyes are dilating, so you can see the risk more clearly, "All the things we think of as long-term priorities are redirected to the immediate interest: fight or flight." Most people may get sweaty and flushed or have cold, clammy hands when they're scared, he says. That's because the flow of blood is away from the outside of the body into the larger muscles of the heart.

"If you're going to fight or run, you want as much blood flow to the body's big muscles," you're probably going to experience a fall in digestive function. Peristalsis, which in the gastrointestinal system is a wave-like motion that regulates digestion, takes a lot of energy, says Evans. So, your body has no time to do that when you decide not to join the Deed's Army.

"All the issues we find to be long-term priorities are redirected to the immediate interest: fight or flight,"

Anxiety is fear gone wrong

The reaction to fear is designed to deal with physical threats that lie ahead. But we are living in a society, and at a time when such risks are quite unusual, Evans says. Instead, the sort of danger we are witnessing is, in fact, more mental or personal.

Yet your brain, which tends to over generalize can't tell the difference, says clinical psychologist Kari Ashley Stephens, Ph.D. It means your mind can respond to something like meeting a job deadline just as it would react to something life-threatening, like a car crash or an earthquake.

Fear is an emotional reaction to something the brain considers to be bad, but it's not dangerous," some of this fear can be good. It protects you by telling you what you need to avoid when something is coming in your way. For example, you won't be killed if you miss a work deadline, but it might cost you your job. And it's not necessarily dangerous to walk outside at night, but having the fear response kick in and telling you to walk with a friend might keep you out of an adverse situation.

Chapter 4: Understanding the Difference between Fear and Phobia

For starters, almost everyone has an unreasonable fear of spiders or your annual dental check-up. These fears are minor for most people. But when fears become so dangerous that they cause tremendous distress and interfere with your regular life, phobias are named.

A phobia is an ultimate fear of something that poses little or no real danger, in fact. Close-in areas, heights, highway driving, flying insects, snakes, and needles are common phobias and fears. But almost anything you can develop phobias. While most phobias emerge in infancy, in later life they may also develop.

If you have a phobia, you may understand that your fear is irrational, but you are still unable to control your feelings. Just think of the entity or circumstance you are afraid of can make you nervous. And the terror is automatic and overwhelming when you're actually exposed to the thing you're scared of. The feeling is so uncomfortable that you can do much to stop it an inconvenience or even change your lifestyle. For example, if you have claustrophobia, if you have to ride the elevator to get to the office, you could turn down a lucrative job offer. If you're afraid of heights, you could drive an additional 20 miles to avoid a big bridge.

The first step in overcoming the phobia is to accept it. Knowing that phobias are common is essential. (Having a phobia doesn't mean you're crazy!) It also allows you to realize that phobias can be handled very well. You will conquer your anxiety and fear and start living the life you want; no matter how uncontrollable it feels right now.

4.1 What is a phobia?

A phobia is a fear that is misplaced and unfounded.

The word ' phobia' is often used to refer to a standard trigger's fear. Nevertheless, the American Psychological Association (APA) identifies three forms of phobia. These include:

Real phobia: this is a particular trigger's extreme, irrational fear.

Public phobia or social anxiety: this is a deep fear of public humiliation and being recognized or viewed in a social situation by others. For someone with social anxiety, the thought of large social events is overwhelming. It's not the same as timidity.

Agoraphobia: It is a fear of situations from which it is hard to escape if a person experienced extreme panic, such as being in a lift or being away from one's home. It is commonly misunderstood as the fear of open spaces, but it could also be used to be restricted to a small space, such as an elevator, or public transport. There is an increased risk of panic disorder in people with agoraphobia.

General phobias are referred to as clear phobias as they can be related to a specific cause that may not always occur in an individual's everyday life, such as snakes. Therefore, these are not expected to have a significant impact on daily living.

Because their symptoms are less easily recognized, social anxiety and agoraphobia are known because of nuanced phobias. It may also be more difficult for people with complex phobias to avoid stimuli, such as being in a crowd or leaving the house.

When a person starts planning their lives around avoiding the source of their fear, a phobia becomes diagnosable. It's worse than a normal reaction of terror. Individuals with phobia need to stop anything that causes their panic by being overwhelmed.

Phobias are more severe than mere feelings of fear and are not limited to specific causes ' fears.

While individuals are aware of the irrational nature of their phobia, they cannot regulate the reaction of fear.

Sweating, chest pain, pins, and needles may be symptoms.

Medication and behavioural therapy may be included in care.

The U.S. has a phobia of 19 million men.

"Natural" fears vs. phobias or "irrational" fears

Experiencing anxiety in dangerous situations is natural and even beneficial. Fear serves a purpose of defence, triggering the automatic response of "fight-or-flight." We can respond quickly and defend ourselves with our bodies and minds alert and ready for action. But the risk is either inexistent or greatly exaggerated with phobias. It's only reasonable, for example, to be terrified of a snarling Doberman, but it's unreasonable to be frightened of a friendly poodle on a leash, as you might be if you've got a dog phobia.

Four common types of phobias and fears exist:

1. Phobias of animals like the fear of snakes, mice, rats, and cats.

2. Phobias of natural environment such as fear of heights, disasters, water, and darkness.

3. Situational phobias (including fear of enclosed spaces) (claustrophobia), walking, driving, tunnels, and bridges.

4. Blood-injection-phobia of trauma, fear of blood, injury, infection, needles, or other medical procedures.

4.2 Fear vs. Anxiety

There may be physical changes in both fear and anxiety. Both of them can trigger the fight or flight response of your body. You may experience a quick heartbeat, sweating, shaking, the tension of the muscle, or shortness of breath. With both, you can find that you are having trouble concentrating. You might think that fear and anxiety are the same when you pay attention to just these types of symptoms. There's a big difference between fear and anxiety, though.

Fear is the product of imminent danger or risk. Anxiety is the result of perceived danger or threat. Suppose you're out of work going home. You're alone and outside its dark. In the bushes, you hear rustling, and you see a dark figure. You feel the tension of your body, the rhythm of your soul, and you think you cannot breathe. There is a threat that is "clear and present." It's fast, authentic, and accurate. You're going through terror.

On the other hand, anxiety is a reaction to potential danger. Suppose you walk down the same street, its dusk this time. There are no noises from the forest, and the only people you see are a family walking in front of you with their dog. Even so, you're beginning to worry that something terrible will happen. You have a similar reaction: your heart starts to pound, your body tenses, you begin to shake. You're going through panic. Nothing has occurred that would signal some risk; the likelihood of danger is your reaction.

Fear plays a protective role in the life of all. Your body alerts you when faced with danger–physical or emotional–and is ready to defend itself against the risk. If you cross a street and a car has driven by suddenly, your fear will help you move quickly to the side of the road. You may still feel the effects of your fear for a few minutes. You may be shaking, and you may need some time to calm down.

Nevertheless, as the risk fades, those emotions will vanish, and you will start your day. Anxiety can come from big moments like someone pointing a gun at you, or small moments like a bee's anxiety of stung. And, whether small or large, the signs of fear disappear when the danger stops.

Anxiety does not automatically dissipate because it comes from a perceived or possible threat. Even though there is no risk, the body remains on high alert. You can find it challenging to carry out daily activities when anxiety tends to flare up. Perhaps you don't want to go down the street at night anymore. If anxiety persists, the fear of your anxiety may grow; you may avoid leaving the house at night, so you're not going to have to walk down any street and worry that somebody will run at you.

Anxiety may cause other issues in addition to having an emotional impact. It wears down the body as depression is constant and chronic. Short bursts of fear may help protect you, but a prolonged state of anxiety can put you at risk of heart disease, stroke, or other physical diseases. For some people, having the ability to categorize their emotions either fear or anxiety may help to look at the situation and reduce anxiety symptoms.

The question is what the difference between trust and fear is? We have an answer to this question already. It was mentioned earlier that, while anxiety is not, fear is often correlated with clear indications.

But this view is not agreed upon by everyone. Simple behaviourists claim that "all anxiety has simple, recognizable signs," even if some are "more subtle than others." They agree that something as ambiguous as "patterns of light and dark" can be viewed as indications.1 However, in contrast to panic, fear is more closely associated with the reaction to battle or flight. Right now, if you're at work and you're living in an unsafe neighbourhood, you might be worried about the possibility of being physically attacked as you go home from work at night. Your physiological responses, which are likely to be mild at the moment, would be better in such an assault if it happened to you; hopefully, it never did.

The length of your response is linked to another way of separating anxiety from fear. Whereas fear "includes rapid and acute response to the imminent threat (i.e., battle or flight), anxiety involves a more persistent, longer-term pattern of vigilance." Another suggested distinction concerns the level of focus: fear is correlated with close attention, but" anxiety is associated with a proactive expansion of awareness to detect threats if they actually exist."

Instead, your attention spreads in anticipation of anxiety. For example, if you feel anxious while at home alone at night, then whenever you hear the ring of the telephone or the wind blowing against the windows, you start scanning your surroundings in anticipation of something coming to pass early.

It also ensures that your depression is likely to stay relatively constant, with small ups and downs as you assess each new stimulus (e.g., ringing phone). On the other hand, the response to terror, fight, or flight elevates rapidly and drastically subsides once the source of fear is removed.

4.3 Fear vs. Worry

We're not feeling the thing at the moment when we're concerned. We're afraid of having the experience, experiencing the feelings we want to avoid... one day.

This worry may feel like a lot of fear. And it can produce similar effects. You're reluctant to go forward, you're indecisive, and you're still hiding from the world. You're not sure if you're supposed to put yourself out there in a new way because there's a risk of failure or ignorance.

Whether its anxiety, worry, or a mixture of both our cognitive, physical and emotional resources can be sapped too much. And there's a lot more we can learn from facing our anxiety, even accepting it.

Everything you've ever wanted is on the other side of fear. "Agree or disagree? The saying means that if you just conquer the fear, you get what you want. Liberated from the anxiety that holds you back, you step confidently and quickly toward your goals. Eradicating fear isn't a requirement to achieving what you're dreaming of and striving for.

It is when you are afraid of the fear itself that there will be issues and obstacles

You automatically switch to avoiding habits that mess up everything when you don't develop a tolerance for a right, reasonable amount of fear. You're worried about getting distracted from feeling the anxiety. To stop yourself from realizing that you are out of reach to certain aspects of life. You're taking a risk to keep yourself from realizing that yes, and yes, you might get hurt. It pretends to be necessary to worry, but it is not constructive, and it is not helpful.

Exploit your worries with your imagination

Worrying is to concentrate your attention on all the negative results at the cost of using the same resources to solve problems. Fears need to be handled through a mixture of tolerance and positive reassurance. The power that you are applying to your thoughts and feelings is what you are feeding your heart.

For your worries, anxiety is junk food. Unlike creative problem solving, welcoming, and attracting help, concern does nothing useful; it only transmits your fears so that your outlook is insular.

For your worries, anxiety is junk food

Worry is full of empty calories, and since you don't give anything useful to digest your anxiety, your fear stays hungry, gorge on your negative thoughts, and ultimately becomes overweight.

Once worries swell from unproductive (i.e., worrying) negative thinking, they are hard to make room for because they are so big; they overpower the emotional landscape. They're too heavy to carry, so they're holding you back from where you're going.

Fear is unavoidable, and anxiety can be stopped.

Fear is profound, and fear is flawed

Fear is intense, and any strength can be positively harnessed. Worry is soft and productively unable to be harnessed.

Fear leads you to personal growth, and heart expansion acceptance of fear is rewarded with greater possibilities. Worry leads you towards insularity and shrinks your ability to connect with others with greater fear, believing worry is "rewarded."

Fear is sound. Worry allows you to become ill.

Everyone is afraid, real or imagined, of something

Find a place to bring them to make sure you control your fears. Invite them to shoot them out instead. During counseling, there is an old saying, pressing in on the thought. Its terror resistance by fear itself, that's the saboteur.

Often fear is intense, particularly as you are transitioning into or out of something. Meeting your fears with effective management is critical during those times. What it feels like is concentrating your attention on creative solutions, confidence, and acceptance. If you need help with this, go ahead and get some assistance. Life's most effective people don't live without fear; because of their fear, they just don't make an enemy.

How to Make Fear your Ally

4.4 Seek help for phobias and fears

Although phobias are rational, they do not always cause significant anxiety or affect your life significantly. For example, if you have a phobia of snakes, and if you live in a place where you are not likely to run into one, it may not cause any problems in your daily activities. On the other hand, living in a big city will pose a problem if you have a severe phobia of crowded spaces.

If your phobia doesn't have that much impact on your life, it's definitely nothing to think about. But if avoiding the object, behavior, or condition that causes your phobia interferes with your normal functioning, or prevents you from doing activities that you would otherwise enjoy, it is time to seek assistance.

Consider treating your phobia if:

- This causes intense and impaired fear, anxiety, and panic

- You understand that your fear is irrational and unfounded

- Because of your phobia, you avoid those circumstances and locations

- Your avoidance interferes with your regular routine or causes severe pain

- You have had phobia for at least six months. What's right for you depend on factors like your phobia's frequency, your exposure to professional therapy, and how much help you need?

Self-help is always worth a try as a general rule. The more you can effort for yourself, the more you will feel in control, which goes a long way in terms of phobias and fears. If your phobia is so severe, however, that it causes panic attacks or uncontrollable anxiety, you may want to seek more help.

Phobias counseling has an excellent track record. Not only it works very well, but you continue to see results very fast, sometimes in as little as one to four sessions. Aid, however, does not have to come in a professional therapist's form. It can be beneficial just to have someone to hold your hand or stand by your side while you face your fears.

Phobia self-help tip 1: Facing your fears

One step at a time, it's only reasonable to want to escape what you're afraid of. But the secret to overcoming phobias is to face your fears. While avoidance in the short term may make you feel better, it prevents you from discovering that your phobia may not be as terrifying or overwhelming as you use to think of it.

We never find the chance to learn how to deal with your worries and take control of the situation. As a result, in your mind, the phobia becomes increasingly frightening and daunting.

The most successful way to overcome a phobia is to expose yourself to what you fear in a safe and controlled manner, slowly and regularly. During this exposure cycle, until it finally passes, you must learn to ride out the anxiety and fear. With repeated encounters facing your anxiety, you will begin to realize that the worst will not happen; you will not die or "lose it." You will feel more confident and in control of each exposure. Phobia is starting to lose its strength.

It's important to start with a situation you can handle and work your way up from there to develop your confidence and coping skills as you move up the "fear ladder." Make a list. Make a list of your phobia-related scary situations. If you are afraid of flying, the list may include: buying your ticket, packing your luggage, driving to the airport, watching planes taking off and land, going through security, boarding the aircraft and listening to the flight attendant give the safety instructions, in addition to the obvious such as taking a flight or taking off.

Create the ladder of your terror

Arrange things from the least terrifying to the most frightening on your list. The first move will make you very nervous, but not so afraid that you are too intimidated to try it out. It will be helpful to think about your end goal when designing the ladder (for example, being able to be near to dogs without panicking) and then break down the steps necessary to achieve that objective.

Make the way up the ladder

Start with the first move, and don't go on until you feel more comfortable doing it. Remain in the situation for as long as possible to reduce the anxiety. The more you expose yourself to the thing you're scared of, the more you're going to get used to it, and the less nervous you're going to feel the next time you face it. You should move on to the next line once you have made a step on several separate occasions without having too much anxiety. If an action is too difficult, break it down or slow down into smaller steps.

The more often you train, the quicker will be your improvement. Don't hurry, though. Go at a pace without feeling overwhelmed that you can handle. And remember: when you confront your doubts, you'll feel uncomfortable and nervous, but the feelings are only temporary. The fear will disappear if you stick with it.

Tip 2: Learn to calm down quickly

When you are nervous or anxious, you experience a variety of painful physical symptoms, such as heart racing and a sense of suffocation. Such physical sensations can be scary and much of what makes the phobia so distressing. Nonetheless, you can become more secure in your ability to tolerate uncomfortable feelings and face your fears by learning how to calm down quickly.

Perform a simple exercise of deep breathing. You tend to take fast, shallow breaths (known as hyperventilating) when you're nervous, which actually contributes to anxiety's physical feelings. You can reverse these physical sensations by breathing deeply from the abdomen and feel less stressed, less out of breath, and less nervous. Practice until you are comfortable with the exercise when you feel calm.

- Sit or stand straight with your back comfortably. Place your neck with one hand and your belly with the other.

- Take a slow nose draw, counting to four. The hook should rise on your stomach. The arm is supposed to move very little on your neck.

- For a count of seven, hold your breath.

- Exhale to eight through your mouth, forcing your abdominal muscles out as much air as you can. The hand on your stomach is supposed to move in as you exhale, but very little will run the other side.

- Repeat the cycle again until you feel relaxed and focused.

- Practice this five-minute twice-day deep breathing technique. You can use it when you are dealing with your phobia or in another stressful situation when you are confident with the method.

Use your senses

One of the simplest, easiest and effective ways to relieve anxiety is to engage the sight, sound, taste, scent, touch, or vibration of one or more of your senses. But since everyone is exceptional, you will have to try to find out what works best for you.

Move: walk, jump up and down, or stretch gently. Relieving anxiety, dancing, drumming, and running can be particularly effective.

Sight: Look at anything that makes you feel happy or smiling: a beautiful view, family pictures, internet cat pictures.

Sound: listen to music relaxing, sing a favorite melody, or play an instrument of music. Or enjoy nature's soothing sounds (both live and recorded): ocean waves, winds through the forest, singing birds.

Smell: candles with a soft fragrance. Smell the greenhouse flowers. Breathe in the fresh and clean air. Spray on the scent of your choice.

Taste: Eat a favorite dish slowly, savoring every bite. Sip a cup of herbal tea or coffee. Chew a gum pin. Love a hard candy mint or your pick.

Touch: Massage yourself with your hand or neck. Cuddle the dog. Wrap in a soft blanket. Lie in the cool breeze outside.

Tip 3: Challenge negative thoughts of your phobia

You may overestimate how bad it will be if you are exposed to the situation you fear and underestimate the ability to cope with when you have a phobia. Usually, negative and unrealistic are the anxious thoughts that cause and intensify phobias. You will start challenging these unhelpful ways of thinking by writing down the negative feelings you have when faced with your phobia. Such reflections also fall into the following categories: telling fate. For example, This Bridge is going to break; I'm going to make a fool of myself for sure; I'm certainly going to lose it when the doors of the elevator close. Once I got a shot, I fainted once. By going out, I will never be able to get a shot again; the pit bull lunged at me. All dogs are dangerous. "Disastrous. We are going through turbulence, said the pilot. The plane will crash! The guy coughed next to me. Perhaps it's swine flu. I'll get very sick!

Chapter 5: Wisdom Conquers Fear

We have a choice in every moment of our lives–to be limited by fear or to live freely. It's the difference between being controlled by the head or the heart, adhering to boundaries, or opening up to limitless possibility.

Fear is the dissuasive to bring about a rewarding, imaginative, and generally impressive existence. Not that with terror, there's anything wrong. It is a natural human emotion that, by defending, directing, and keeping things safe, looks out for us. And that's just what we need sometimes.

Yet we play it small when fear is in charge, and our vision is constrained. Whether we're conscious about it or we are not, we live in a self-defined box labeled "the same," ignoring the possibility of what's fresh, exclusive, and potentially extremely satisfying.
The inner wisdom also nudges us toward a greater, freer, and more expansive. It shows up in unconventional ways–the spontaneous thoughts about what you'd love to do, the feeling of excitement that comes from nowhere, the "Yeah!" When you get involved with an idea, person, operation, or circumstance, you feel like that. It may also whisper the truth about what in your life does not work.

5.1 Inner Wisdom Triggers Fear

For fear, moving internal knowledge towards the surface is a warning to go on alert. The part of us wired to survive feels threatened when we are forced to shift, step out of our comfort zone, and test the waters of the unknown. It's like the inner sentry just had their weapons cocked, ready to defend themselves against the enemy.

It is necessary to bring our fear into the light of day if we want to create the space to express our gifts and passions. And it helps to unlock our inner wisdom. Learn to negotiate these roads that seem to be discordant, and fear will lose its power over you.

Get to know fear

Although, with time, fear can diminish, it is unlikely to disappear completely. Think of coping as a lifestyle of anxiety. The goal of getting to know fear is not to remove it, but to become aware of it so that it can be understood and recognized. It may come up a million times more, but if you're open to working with it rather than running from it, you can start finding your way through it with a little ease.

• Our minds devise every possible (and not so probable) negative outcome so that we do not step forward.

• We've got feelings full of self-doubt–I can't, I can't, and I'm not expected to.

• We're feeling nervous and stressed.

• We're concerned.

• Maybe we're tired.

• We're not going to take a chance.

• We're frozen, afraid of moving.

• In familiar territory, we want to live.

• We want to keep a check.

All about shielding us from the unknown is the sense of terror. Ironically, fear wants us to stay on familiar ground, even if we are not helped by the situation in life or the pattern of thought we carry out. But when the time is ripe to let go of the present, something in us knows.

Get to Know Inner Wisdom

If we listen to the inner voice that speaks the truth within us, we are invited or compelled to proceed out into the unknown, take a risk, and try something new. The wisdom that passes into us is not about survival, but about development and possibility. It's not about security or defense. It doesn't understand the boundary meaning. It is relentlessly innovative because it has no interest in the mechanisms of the mind that clamp down on our thought.

Fear of risk? Will there be self-doubt? Do you have to feel in control? These have no significance to our inner wisdom's boundless existence.

Be prepared to meet the feeling of not knowing if you dip your toe into the waters of your authentic voice. Recognize you just don't know. Then wait, give up, trust. You understand that anything is possible when the reality of not knowing becomes clear to you. Ideas that you would never pop into your head. Chance encounters are opening doors to incredible opportunities. Help and support come from around the world.

Fear is a genuine emotion common to a human being's life. Fear is bound to emerge if we let our inner wisdom speak. Don't freak out when it does. Take your time. Be curious about how it affects you and what it is like. Receive it with love in an ocean. Let all your past stories unravel that hold it in place.

Turn to and respect your fear experience. Turn away from how it holds you back. Your inner wisdom hits you right now on your shoulder. Are you ready to listen?

5.2 The Three Vital Keys to Unlocking Yourself from Fear

"What scares you, master you." If you're still being dominated by fear, this post will be for you. We all know that a life driven by fear is not working. It keeps us small and confined and takes away our full and glorious creative expression from the world.

It feels terrible to live in terror–have you experienced it? "I can't" and "I shouldn't "-fuelled choices just bring uncertainty and disappointment to our lives. We lose focus, let go of our hopes, and consider it as good enough to be mediocre.

It's not a way of living

Indeed, fear is terrifying. It's getting big. We fear that men, income, health, reputation will be lost. We're afraid to be reckless or lose it all. Despite curiosity, opportunity, and hope, we choose to play it safe. That's you?

Many of us are in a life driven by fear. We were persuaded that we actually couldn't take the risk of putting aside the doubts and moving forward. So, here's the solution: to be afraid we will take an ingenious approach.

It's not enough to suggest that you have to banish or conquer fears. You have to break it down and grasp it from the inside out when it comes to terror. You need to habituate to yourself with how it happens in your environment and develop a lifestyle that keeps you alert and aware so that it doesn't sneak up on you.

How to Make Fear your Ally

It requires commitment and willingness to tackle fear. Want to free yourself out of fear? Then take these three essential keys seriously into account.

Key #1: Get to Know the Fear face

You're not always going to strike by terror head-on. Once we knew that it was driving us, we had many signs of anxiety for years. And it all changed until we did.

The rational response to fear begins by understanding it. And here are the clues:

Obsessive thinking

Excessive mental activity that attempts to evaluate any point of the situation

Doubt and indecision' should or should not?"

Low stress or anxiety, particularly in your body

Living in your brain disconnected from your body. Maybe it feels like this: if you have any of these symptoms, be curious. Look deeply into your past; you're going to see the root of fear. That's good news!

It is essential to understand the face of fear if you want it to lose its power over you.

Why exactly is fear? To free you from terror, the answer to this question is fundamental.

If we tell ourselves a frightening story and feel other body sensations, such as stress or contraction, we experience what we call terror. Keep this knowledge alive for you in your own life–right now–by trying it out. You will find a reaction of fear that occurs in your body as well as thoughts that doubt, worry, evaluate, ruminate, prepare, create, etc.

Congratulations! You've just shone the torch on terror directly. You see that there are physical sensations and anxious, anxiety-producing thoughts every time you feel fear.

Through your exposure to them, these feelings are reinforced, and they keep you trapped in fear. They don't have to be logical or not even real.

So instead of going over and over these feelings (a formula for continued unhappiness), bring your attention directly to the physical sensations in your body. Open the knowledge of what you feel in your body to obtain the experience. Breathe and let it be, even if it's painful.

You have disempowered the doubt at the moment of doing that. You've diverted your attention from the emotions, and you're just with the physical sensations.

This is the time of liberty. You have to unlock the door to freedom from fear when you feel the body sensations without the weight of the nervous thoughts.

Key #3: It's All About the Moment

Learning that the aim is not to get rid of fear is really necessary. What's the reason? To help you on the path to freedom, we want to be very realistic and practical.

Yet independence does not mean that there is no terror. This means working with your background intelligently and anxiety won't control you anymore.

Each time you encounter anxious feelings until you develop a pattern of experiencing the body sensations, fear literally loses its oomph. This softens as you step away from thinking and into the body's sensations.

Apply these moments, and here's what you're going to notice: calmer, more insight about people and situations, more options you've never thought about before, more lightness and happiness in your being.

The only time you can intelligently do anything about anxiety is when it comes at the moment. Stop, relax, feel when you hear it. Each time the key to freedom is turned.

Now What?

As you know, you're confused by terror. This shades your perception to the extreme and, in any case, leaves you blind to the full range of possibilities. And it's holding you closed.

Keys 1, 2, and 3 allow you to let go of anxious thoughts and breathe right in your body with the physical sensations.

It may be present when fear no longer pushes you, but so is your inherent wisdom. You understand the terror, see the reality of it just thoughts and feelings, and step forward liberated and free.

5.3 10 Great Ways Mindfulness Turns Fear into an Ally

You may not bring perception and fear together at first sight, or you may assume that one can counterbalance the other. But while consciousness encourages us to be present with fear instead of running away from it, it also liberates us from being trapped in negative thoughts and feelings.

You may not bring perception and fear together at first sight, or you may assume that one can counterbalance the other. But while consciousness encourages us to be present with fear instead of running away from it, it also liberates us from being trapped in negative thoughts and feelings. Mindfulness, just as it is, causes fear to be without absorption. It transforms fear into an ally that we can use to be bold and fearless.

We all know well what it feels like to fear, how it can surface as an invading adversary when you are least aware of it or join without being invited. It may occur as a natural response to physical danger, but it is self-created more often than not, such as fear of failure, not being good enough, being alone, or the future. For fear of being rejected, being compassionate for fear of leaving, or expressing our feelings for fear of appearing vulnerable, we fear love, and we are easily get controlled by insecurity and self-doubt.

The immediate effect of fear is turning away our feelings of the heart. Let your body take the sensation of being afraid for a moment. What's your stance? Many people hunch their shoulders inward, spread their arms over their chests, or take a similarly defensive stance. The heart goes out of control in this self-protected position, and we cannot feel love or even friendliness. Try to say with real meaning, "I love you," when your arms are tightly folded over your face. Hard to do!

Yet love spreads and opens where fear contracts and closes the heart. Loving is letting go of fear, in other words. So, take the love attitude now. See the reaction of your body, your arms reach out, embrace, and invite. Fear may still be there, but it can be accepted by love, where fear blocks love, love tenderly retains fear. Try to say, "I'm terrified" with your arms stretched wide, and mean it. Difficult to do!

Ten ways mindfulness both influences and transforms fear:

1. You make friends with yourself and the world by carefulness, just as it is.

2. Obviously, friendship contains more goodness, compassion, and affection, the antidotes to fear.

3. Friendship is also the key to greater clarity, simplicity, and tolerance.

4. Carefulness shuts off your nervous system's stress response by triggering the parasympathetic nervous system's calming response; this helps you to stay focused and calm, whatever happens.

3. You are better able to deal with what's happening in a real and present state than if you're stressed or overwhelmed.

6. Anxiety drives you out of your body, restricting your emotions, and bringing your thoughts to a standstill while being conscious keeps you in contact with yourself.

7. Anxiety will shorten and slow the breathing while breathing awareness holds the diaphragm open and deep breath.

8. Mindfulness helps you to see that anxiety is a fleeting emotion that comes and goes, or any other negative feeling.

9. Fearless is not a rejection of fear; it is not a state of being without fear, but one of being conscious.

10. That's right. Fearlessness is recognizing fear, calling it, and taking it by hand to make it your friend and ally.

Do you remember times when you felt fear and pushed through it, times when there was fear, but you kept going? These are periods of anxiety. Fear can close the eyes, but bravery comes from the heart, from the release of resistance. Fear may keep you from being fully involved in life, but fearlessness gives you the confidence to plunge into the unknown.

Fear comes, breathe, and let go; fear comes up, replace it with love; fear knocks at the door, invite it to share a cup of tea. You thus become a brave heart fighter, unshakable, optimistic, and cheerful, with fear as your ally.

Chapter 6: How (and Why) to Make Fear Your Friend

Are you in love with fear? That may sound impossible, but I can promise this learning to be at peace with fear will change your life completely. I don't say you're never going to feel fear again, because it's a natural part of human existence. You're also going to find out that fear has something to tell you. But, if you feel anxiety, you'll know how to be with it so it's not going to run your life. Once we know intimately, fear is in control of our lives once we encourage ourselves to invite it in as a friend. And if we can sleep with terror, it really becomes our ally, not our enemy.

"What You Fight Persists" Talking of the adversary, many of the techniques that we often use to deal with fear perceive it as an opposing force that needs to be taken into account. We're trying to overcome it, move it through, fight it, conquer it, stop it, cope and control it. It sounds like a great deal of work. What is common to these approaches is resistance: in an effort to eradicate or regulate it, we push toward our history of fear. Only gentle techniques, such as deep breathing and soothing self-talk, although sometimes helpful, build anxiety when trying to get rid of fear. No matter how qualified we are to use any of these techniques, there is no question that the anxiety will grow again, demanding more of our precious energy. As the saying goes, "what you resist remains." It comes from the martial art of aikido to step with Fear a guide to an alternative, safe way to address fear. Aikido's ideology is to blend with the attacker's motion rather than face it head-on. We all know how to face fear head-on, but how to balance with its movement?

For some reason I've never truly understood that people are afraid. All that is required is a slight sign of fear, and our bodies and minds are going into hyper drive to try to eliminate it as if fear is an unwelcome intruder, an enemy that is about to kill us. The one and only way to find out if this is true is to stop running and turn around in order to deal with anxiety.

This perpetuates fear, isolation, and discomfort to prevent or ignore our inner perceptions that are actually here. It's like taking an apple pie and tossing a slice out of it because we don't want it to be there. Once we thoroughly know our experiences, they cease to have the power to control us. We are integrated and confident, and finally we can put down our protection and separation vigilance and arms.

The Process of Experience

If you've piqued your curiosity and are willing to start learning fear truly, turn your attention inward. It begins with a very simple greeting: "Hi, fear." The meeting comes from a place where there is transparency, curiosity and not awareness. This may be the first time, after all, that you are really embracing the buddy who could have been your companion for a very long time. Realize that you don't really know what fear is like as much as you may have strategized in the past.

There is also a need for tenderness. Fear may have been the intimate one, the unknown relative, left out in the cold. The melting of the ice needs warm and loving attention because of the fear of coming out of hiding and being seen for what it is which is far less frightening than anything you might imagine.

See how your body feels when you start with, "Hello, fear." Tension, vibration, or flutter may be observed. Resist the urge to suppress the feelings and just remain with them, allowing them to be there without doing anything to them. Don't be afraid. All that's going on is you experience a few physical changes in your body. Just let them do it, and stick with it.

Please note your thoughts. You'll see that they don't describe who you are when you observe them. The thoughts ' witness is kind and open, so you can just let the thoughts be. What they're doing doesn't matter; just let them come and go.

Listen

You are free, accessible, and nudged in welcoming fear (or any other experience). Spiritual teacher Jean Klein says, "You're in a state of listening." There's nothing to do, strategize or exploit, there's no need for the experience to end, not to restrict it in any way just a kind and gentle note of what's true right now. This is a radical way to be with an apparently hard feeling and removes the pain, resistance, and commitment.

You may become aware of a story about it as you are with the experience of fear, as in, "I am afraid of..." The true therapy of actually meeting fear is devoid of the tale it is meeting the fear itself without any substance. Experiment with letting go of the feelings about it and paying attention to what actually happens.

Inquire

Now, let's go deeper by asking questions about the terror. There are a few ideas here: why are you here? What are you trying to tell or what are you trying to do to me?

Hint: You can find that you are trying to protect or empower you with fear.

How are you watching the world? What are you waiting for from people and situations?

How to Make Fear your Ally

Hint: Caution, distrust, doubt, or fear may be found.

You'd like to tell me anything else?

Hint: It's just available.

Taking a while to let soak in what you've heard. Let your heart be open to respecting the fear is present for a cause and has affected and guided you based on your view of the world. You do something so incredible–you encourage a hidden part of you to be seen and heard from the shadows. It is no longer confined to your unconscious where you are annoyed and stressed. It is warmly welcomed to emerge as a valid and true one.

The Mystery of Not Knowing

What is happening is part of the mystery at this stage? Through welcoming terror, as we end the inner war and put down our weapons, we are in a situation that we have never been before. Allow the room for understanding to come and listen to you in the vacuum of not knowing. If the spark appears to make any adjustments, have the courage to follow it, as it is the natural path in life, not one based on fear and limitation.

I can't stress enough this last point, and that's to always open your heart to completely face the terror. Just as good health requires a unique lifestyle of consideration for diet and exercise, being comfortable with anxiety requires a willingness to meet it directly. Unless you accept the encounter so it's going to go away, it's actually not going to go away as you still resist. But if, as it is, you're open to anything that happens, you'll find it doesn't matter whether or not there's fear. Life is so prosperous. Any subsequent experience is a friend, a gift, an opportunity to break down your inner boundaries. Allow all in all, and you'll find peace beyond peace.

6.1 Steps to Kicking Fear in the Teeth & Making it Your Ally

While our greatest nemesis is often considered to keep us from achieving more, what if fear were your greatest teacher that could make you unstoppable?

 a nine-step process to use every day to remove the old conditioning you have around fear and make it your most effective ally from being your enemy.

While we may want to improve our lives and increase our success, fear drives many of our decisions.

Most of our fears, unfortunately, are not based on logic or truth. It's not true. Of course, the feeling of fear is very real and I definitely don't deny that. Fear is just another sense of joy, rage, disappointment, anticipation, or sorrow. Often these feelings cause a physiological reaction. Like these other sensations, the response of our body to the feeling of fear is expressed in a variety of ways; an accelerated pulse or rhythm, temporary paralysis, a knot in our stomach, arms, or back, or even suddenness.

In reality, there are two sections that make up the fear experience. Such two pieces, however, are often combined together. When one aspect of fear is the feeling of fear, the other element of fear is the one we fear, or the cause that sends us to fear.

Since most of us collapse together what we fear and the feeling of fear without distinguishing between these two pieces, we tend to resist fear and make it our enemy rather than accept fear as an ally.

The three points in time we are all acquainted with: the past, the present and the future. What we are afraid of is just the negative expectation or perception of what will go to happen in the future (what we never want to do) and what never happens in the present.

If we are forced to avoid consequences or what we don't want to do, we are pulled in the opposite direction to what we want; enjoyment. Since fear is the pessimistic expectation of the result, try to shift the attention to the positive outcome or what you want to manifest rather than what you want to prevent.

This is the key point here; our fears are as "true" as our dreams are! But as long as we give more strength to our fears than to our dreams, our fears will always feel as if they are more of a truth and in effect will make us better. When you stop for a moment and think about it, they are both dreams and images of a future that we have created or visualized in the frame of our mind. The same method is used to build both our fears and dreams; our imagination!

The problem is that most of us spend more time dwelling on what we fear rather than on what we want to create goals or dreams. Let's face it; we're all pretty good at articulating what we don't want to do in our lives while trying to get a vivid picture of what we want or our aspirations and dreams.

When you know what you don't want and don't know what you want, where do you think you're going to wind up your thoughts and energies continuously? There's not even a shot for your goals and dreams! Alternatively, inspire your dreams and goals to be the driving force that drives you forward, rather than your fears. Once you do that, you'll be able to make the most of what you want.

Imagine if you welcomed fear and found it one of your biggest instructors, what would be possible? When you avoid fear or respond when you feel fear, you will not be able to learn from it or understand any lessons that would lead to your continued personal development. And if you don't learn from it, you can't see fear as something that can be re-framed into a constructive opportunity to grow so improve.

Take time to think about how much of your life is dominated by fear and your decisions. To begin to decide whether fear is a realistic threat or just your active imagination, the next time you feel yourself responding to fear or feel the tight hold that fear can have on you, take the following nine steps to control your life's fear and make it your ally. In this way, you can improve your relationship with fear and learn to respond to it in a healthier way rather than responding and surrendering all of your personal power to fear continuously.

1. Give Yourself Permission to Feel the Fear

If you feel the feeling of fear overcoming you, rather than freezing or resisting the experience of fear, encourage yourself to experience the feeling of fear.

Instead of looking at fear as a "stop sign," encourage yourself to consider fear as a source of important information by saying to yourself, "Okay, I'm afraid." You'll find that fear is simply a sensation and will begin to dissipate until you announce and fully experience it. That way, instead of letting it persist eternally, you can get it through.

2. Breathe!

This affects our breathing pattern when we feel fear, tension, concern, anxiety, or excitement. We start breathing irregularly. Take a few long, slow breaths to stop this. In the nose and out through the ears. This exercise alone will calm you down, alleviate anxiety, stop your hands from trembling, increase your heart rate, and get you back to the present situation quickly.

3. Learn

Recognize this as a chance to grow and learn. "Okay, the fear shows up to teach you something so let's discuss it further. Is the fear telling me that you need additional information, tools, services, and training? Is there a small expectation that you hold on to? Is there a potential outcome that you want to avoid? Are you trying to play it safe?"

4. it's not real

Embrace this feeling by saying, "I feel a fear here that's not happening right now. While the feeling of the fear is very real and you are experiencing that feeling right now, what I'm really afraid of is not real because it's focused on a possible negative future outcome that hasn't happened yet!"And,' I'm scared of something that happened in the past that I didn't want to happen and I'm afraid it's going to happen again so I'm taking a past experience and implementing it into the future as the negative intention of what I don't want to do.'

5. Take Control

Regardless of what you don't want or want to stop, shift your focus to the result you want to build or manifest. Create in your mind the vivid image. Look at the positive future result you want to achieve and guide your thoughts. Tell yourself, "What do I want to build for myself in this situation now that I know what I don't want or what I'm trying to avoid?"(For example: happy customers, an improvement in my income, more opportunities to support others, stronger abilities, better relationships, greater confidence, greater consistency, success in my career, a positive person, achieving my target, etc.)

6. Take Action

Now that the outcome you want to produce has been established, what steps will you take to achieve this outcome? Consider this if you're staring at a pile of paper, a call list, a survey, or a project you need to complete that causes your paralysis. Take a piece of paper (or on your computer) and just start listing the steps, one by one, of what you feel you need to do to complete each task or to accomplish / surpass what you're afraid of in your pile of' do's.' Don't think about whether or not your steps are' perfect.' Just doing this will allow you to take action that will eliminate the pressure and make the task more challenging. If you're still lost, ask for help with your measures in practice. Chances are, rather than the steps you need to take to reach the end result, you're concentrating more on getting to the end result. Alternatively, concentrate on the operation. I promise that you will not only get closer to your target after every single step you take, but that you will find the anxiety subsides when you take every small step. Your mission or target will be done before you know it! Finally, the next time it happens, you have a system to deal with this terror.

7. Be Present

How to Make Fear your Ally

Redirect your thoughts and energies in time back to the present moment and what is actually going on in the present as opposed to a potential prediction or past experience. The negative result, or what you are afraid of, is what comes next. It's not what's going on now. You can't be there if you feel fear and if you're in the present moment, you can't experience fear!

Everything you fear is always going to happen in the future and is never going to happen in the present moment. This is the real advantage here. Instead of thinking about the negative assumptions of the future, if you can live in the present moment, anxiety won't be able to touch you.

8. Time for an Upgrade

Finally, how can you upgrade your confidence in this fear? If this fear emerges again, how can you change your thinking to improve and teach you something to step forward and forge ahead instead of causing you to be frozen and consumed by fear?

Make your ally afraid. Embrace the idea that it is trying to teach you something if and when you feel fear. Enable yourself to feel fear in order to grow beyond it. In a healthier way, reacting to fear will give you the opportunity to grow and learn, leading to greater knowledge and unparalleled results. Not only that, but you're going to become stronger, more optimistic, and more focused on your goals.

View fear as your loop of emotional input or as an internal learning barometer. In simple words, our bodies react when we are in physical pain and let us know. It's a sign of danger or we might be sick or wounded. That's the actual feedback loop of our body. When we neglect the pain very often, it gets even worse. Alternatively, we can choose to do something about it by remembering the pain.

Reflect more on what's now rather than what's next the real power is at present rather than having everything to drag us into the future, including our ambitions or sales targets. Be cautious not to live in the future, but to live in the present by concentrating more on what is now rather than what is next. You will find that your worries will lose their powerful edge as you focus on the present and on your desired outcomes, beliefs and personal vision.

Be mindful of these two conflicting truths. Be mindful of your objectives while at the moment you're engaged.

6.2 Reasons Why Fear Is Your Greatest Ally

As kids, we might have been terrified of a creature living in the closet. Or we might have looked up from something that caught our attention at the mall to realize unexpectedly that our mother was in sight nowhere! We may have been afraid to read in front of the class in school, or perhaps we were afraid to take a stand for ourselves when confronted by the bully of the school.

When we're young, our best coping strategy is to avoid the situations that cause fear. We turn the light on, cling to the hand of our mother as she pushes us down the aisle past all the interesting items, get sick on the day we're supposed to share our science project, or avoid the playground.

But as an adult, we might suddenly remember that if we were not afraid of public speaking, we would like to lead the group. And maybe we'd like to camp with our families, if only being in the dark woods wasn't that scary.

As a self-proclaimed neurologist, I spent a lot of time exploring fears and finding ways of manipulating them. We don't really need to avoid the circumstances which make us uncomfortable. We may develop other strategies to cope with fears of all kinds quickly. When we realize that anxiety is not something we need to "fear," we immediately have all sorts of options to live our lives more fully in all the ways we want. Yes, your fears may be your greatest allies. This is why:

1. The edges of your boxes are shown by terror. The typical reaction to fear is turning and running the other direction. As such, our safe zone is characterized by fears. Looking at my life, I can see that I like to live in places where there is no danger. This gives me a home, a place where I can feel safe and comfortable. But beyond that box of protection lies a lot of life and experience. If we want to experience life entirely, we're going to want to move on those fears.

2. Their false identities may be exposed to terror. Most people believe there is a basic characteristic that determines who they are. While this may be valid, most of our identities are characterized not by our essence, but by our weaknesses. A fear of water may prohibit me from swimming in the ocean or in the lake while enjoying a holiday. I can even tell its a given to myself. I'd rather stay dry and clean instead of dirty and dusty. I can just agree to be a land-lover. It's that I'm. I may consider it as well. I've heard a lot of customers tell me they're shy. They're who they are. But if we look closer, we can see that there is no meaning of being named "shy." Rather, we're all terrified of being seen. Once we understand the concerns point to our limits and do not determine our personalities, we begin to have some wiggle room to expand our options, push beyond the boundaries of our boxes, and experience more flexibility in our lives.

3. Fear alone is just an illusion. We still view fear as a "fact." We have to conquer it, change it, and overcome it. At most, fear can be a cascade of chemical reactions in our body loosened by abstract thought or physical threat. But there is no substance to fear itself. We view as a phenomenon the cascade of chemical reactions. Yet there is nothing out there, beyond us that can be named or branded "fear." It is an excellent first step to be able to use it to your benefit and know that fear is not something out there that can harm you. If you feel scared, just explore the illusion. Imagine the terror before you. It may be a ghost, or a cloud of deep, gloomy smoke. Go in the direction of it. Let it get you surrounded. Speak to it. It deals with it. You will quickly notice that fear itself is not something frightening, but a smoke and mirror illusion. You're too well on your way to making an ally out of your fears with this experience.

4. Fear still divides us from things that are incredibly good. When I learned that fear is an illusion and that it just shows me my limits, I set out confidently to travel whenever my fears emerged. The most surprising thing about this experience of confronting my fears regularly was that I have always found behind those fears the greatest gifts that have enriched my life tremendously. This gift has often been far beyond anything that I can foresee or dream of. Imagine how our lives become enriched when fear no longer blocks our imagination, our passion, and our possibilities!

5. Fear is not your tyrant; it needs to be your friend. It was originally designed to save your life the cascade of chemical responses in our body! If you need to run for your life or leap out of a charging bull's way, you want that to happen. Fear in this sense has always been our friend. Yet we later developed a sense that there was something out there to fear, to terrorize and intimidate us.

It has become the nemesis of us. Depending on our viewpoint, something to beat, or something to hinder us. But it makes a good friend like that! Now we get curious when we are afraid! What's the limitation? In this direction, what gifts are hidden? To lead us into my next growth, we depend on our fear. And it never let us down yet!

Exercise: Fear-Busting Rehearsal Our body is programmed to respond with a cascade of responses when something scares us. We call this set of responses "fight or flight." The physical body does not know the difference between a real or imaginary situation when visualizing it, so it reacts as if the situation is appropriate.

We can use this propensity to change our response to something that usually gives rise to fear. This is a way for us to face our anxiety before the actual event: somehow visualize the situation that causes fear as much as possible in detail.

Note where there is an emotion of fear. We sometimes find it in their lungs, their intestines, their ears, but it can be anywhere.

Take rational sentiment. How do you neutralize an emotion? Choose from a variety of ways: Move your consciousness through discomfort; untangle the feeling until it subsides; consider the direction in which the feeling travels and push in the opposite direction; or Focus on your breathing until it subsides.

Using the above to play before you find out what works for you.

Return your mind to imagining and replay the case.

Note how the next time you visualize it, the fear is different. Start until you feel that you have no fearful emotion!

Perhaps this will only take you once, or ten times, or 100 times. Try to see how special it is every time. It has been my understanding that it will take fewer repetitions as you get used to changing things in this way.

6.3 Please Don't Let Fear Limit You

Whether we let self-doubt or feelings of inadequacy keep us from recognizing our potential, or embrace the fact that our potential is infinite when we turn our attention away from ourselves.

1. There's no target

Comprehend profoundly that the aim is not to get rid of fear. It's always. Fear may go away for a while, but if it comes back, don't be put off. Each time you see it as a chance. Repeat the holy acceptance mantra, "Yeah, this," and step forward with anxiety rather than exclusion.

2. Stop the fight

Instead of fighting against it, take the attitude of working with terror. Think of an aikido master who is moving with his opponent's energy to gain power. The power comes from putting the fight down and enabling the existence of fear.

3. Story's end

Understanding that telling a terror story strengthens the sensation. Note the self-talk inside. If it tells terrifying tales about the future, the guilty is terror. Alternatively, bring your attention directly to the sensation. It just does not help to repeat stories based on fear.

4. It is intelligence that is supreme

The intimate knowledge of fear in every moment it occurs. Know what causes it, note it, see how it works in your body, and change how it affects your emotions and behavior. Be an expert in terror, so you're no longer oppressed.

5. Launch the Internal Revolution, One Moment at a Time

If we can't find the truth right where we are, where else are we waiting to find it?"Perhaps we complicate this road of inner peace more than it needs to be.

- We agree that we have to work hard to get rid of the thoughts and feelings that are bothering us.

- When we appear to be stuck in structured trends, we conclude that we have not made any progress.

- When we fight, we'll find that we're never going to be happy and awake.

- We have all sorts of ideas to achieve peace and they just aren't effective.

Such thoughts are a mind's inventions that take you away from what you really want. We snatch your focus from your present moment experience's sacred unfolding.

The only moment you're hurting is now, and with painful emotions and messy memories, the only way you can find peace now.

You won't find happiness if you expect the past will improve or if you want a better future. These are mental gestures away from this moment that will keep you feeling as if you lack what you need to be content with.

On the contrary, we are starting the inner revolution, one moment at a time

It takes just a second to invite when you know that you are spinning in a programmed pattern in a slow and aware breath.

For endless love and care, it doesn't take any time to turn inward.

This is the cycle of waking, and it is one moment at a time.

You don't have to worry about changing who you are or finding out how all your problems can be solved. It's so much easier the real path to peace and it boils down to the moment.

- Stop feeding fluster stories about ourselves and others;
- Open up to physical sensations and energies that emerge in the body;
- Check in with our five senses and turn our attention back to the present;
- Rest in the still, endless space of compassion that keeps all in love.

That's what changes it all. We now have a modern, honest and true relationship with the moment.

The mind will tell you that it's not enough to find freedom at the moment. You will be blamed for not consistently training or doing it correctly. But this is not valid.

Only take a moment to turn inward. Then perhaps one more lately in the day or the day after. Then another, Begin the inner revolt, whenever you know, turning inside.

It's as simple as finding inner liberty... one moment at a time.

6. Ending the Internal War of Resisting Your Experience

"What you resist doesn't just endure but increases in scale." It's our natural, awakened state to resist something.

When the idea of separation is removed, there is actually the free flow of perception that constantly embraces everything.

There is no danger, no fear, and no sense to escape or protect a human. It's easy.

Yet add to human reactions, fears, wishes, and aspirations, and the universe splits into inner and outer duality, acceptable and unacceptable otherwise known as human suffering.

If you want to know your true nature's luminous harmony, then learn how and when to resist.

What is being resisted? It is an irritated mind operation that says a resounding, "NO!"Learn at the moment. It's a tendency to stick to some memories and push away others a desire to make things different from what they are.

Take a moment to reflect:

- What are your feelings?

- Where do you say no to what is actually happening in your life?

- Where do you want things to be different than they are or intend them to be different?

Somebody recently wrote to me saying she hates the way she feels with too much anxiety and too many anxious feelings when she wakes up in the morning.

Hating is resisting the perception, and resisting is a stuck feeling formula.

You're stuck in a struggle with what's going on, leaving no room to change or push the experience itself. Resisting invigorate the experience rather than giving it the freeing space without attachment that it needs to come and go.

We are masters of our experience resisting. How are you going to reject? Here are some possibilities:

• Compelling behaviors such as overeating, excessive use of alcohol or drugs, excessive shopping, texting or gossiping

• Being too distracted or worried to be present with your life

- Recycling feelings of anxiety, judgment, frustration or blame

- Resenting how you feel

- Waiting for or hoping that things would improve the popular reason behind all these behaviors if your own knowledge is an adversary, how can you possibly know the peace of your true nature?

7. What's the substitute?

You make the divine choice to stop the momentum from the outside, slow things down, and turn inward with devotion. Changes now have space to change as you create a new, loving relationship with what is changing.

You're polite, accessible, and curious, rather than hating what's going on. You're letting things be like they are. You become the welcome force with your experience that ends the inner war.

Why don't you try it so you know what it feels like? Just go inward and say hello to any emotions, feelings, or physical sensations that are there, warm and loving. The mind is silent as the one who wants to fight begins to fall apart. With no focus in your thoughts to the plot, you're one with what looks like, loving it with a warm cuddle like a long-lost child coming home.

And you're like awakened consciousness here- vibrant, free, and resisting nothing.

Chapter 7: Did You Ever Think That Fear Could Improve Your Life?

If we build the capacity to accept it, everything that belongs to us comes to us. We could get used to it as well as learn to love it. Fear is a common part of a human being, a growing emotion. The better we learn about terror, because awareness is king. Once we turn to face it, get acquainted with it and stop running away, fear is losing its control over us. Would you like to control yourself, or would you like to be a fear victim? It's as simple as that.

Ask yourself if you could say a few more things about when and how to listen to and respond to the messages of a specific fear, how to deal with the intuition behind fear, and when it's easier not to let fear control you. When do you give the wind caution and go for it and trust that it will work out vs. regulating my action based on fear concerns?

A Brief First on Fear

The desire to be frightened is coded into our Genes. They are wired for survival and the brain is on alert when that survival is threatened and the nervous system is excited. This is known as the reaction to the fight or flight. In this physiological response, we humans add an explanation and the sense in which it occurs, marking it as fear. So, this is what fear is: in the mind, physical symptoms and a name.

If you are a gazelle pursued by a cheetah, it makes perfect sense to feel threatened and go into fight or flight. But what if you're worried that your partner will abandon you or miss a deadline? You may respond by trying to think your way out of the situation, but the basic physiological reaction and urge to fight or fly is no different from that of the gazelle.

In addition to security

Yet we all know that we are better than the essence of our species. We are blessed with the ability to dream, to hope and to be happy for a fulfilling life. We may reach an inner awareness. We're smart and creative. We love awe, wonder, and pleasure.

These encounters go beyond living. They are in the process of growth and upgrading. Although life is restricted to the physical body, they are boundless and everlasting. Maybe we could call them spiritual.

Fear is a friend of yours

So, here's the shame. We are in a physical body that experiences fear, but we want so much more than we are given by fear. We are fearful that we will not succeed, but we are eager to grow beyond measure.

When we disregard the impulse and give in to fear, we end up in misery and disillusionment, believing that life needs to have more. We're right–that's it! And if we disregard fear, we are still driven by it.

There is only one solution if fear is present but we want to communicate our full potential: to learn fear. Only then, instead of survival, can we choose the desire of our heart, boundlessness rather than contraction.

Not that survival is incorrect, which is why fear can teach us some valuable things. Once we see that our fear is no longer the enigmatic beast that we claim the gifts it gives us come to light.

Fear counteracts the momentum

The reason for fear, as we have now known, is survival. Fear is paralysing in its pure form (think terror). This forbids us to move forward by motivating the mind to project every possible negative result, even though we cannot know what will happen until it does.

We have the opportunity to see its worth until we relax in the face of fear. We should pause and take a breath when we're afraid. Instead we understand the fear tells us to hesitate, to exercise caution, to look at alternatives before we run.

Often jumping in is the right thing to do, but you can do it with a sage's thoughtfulness and understanding by harnessing the power of fear?

Is it a fear or arousal?

Everything we call terror, together with a mental and situational understanding of fear, is a certain physiological reaction–pounding pulse, body stress, and sweating, upset stomach. Experiment with removing the fear mark. There's an anticipation physical response, but is it fear? Maybe you're shocked. Perhaps it's stimulation, excitement or passion.

Look ahead of your thoughts identifying the emotion of fear immediately. You can find an underrated gem here to help you.

Fear is the passion that inspires.

When we trace fear back to its source, we will eventually find a place that feels unloved inside ourselves. Most fears run unconsciously because we did not get the love and tenderness that we wanted when we were afraid or hurting at some point during childhood.

Happiness is the emotional pain treatment. Take your mind to your own heart and discover love's infinite strength. Then let the frightened young man who lives inside you wash it. Feel it over and over like an infinite waterfall.

So many advantages here, you are caring, you love, and you are healing. And once the fear is no longer separate from the renowned whole of you, the best course of action can be carefully chosen.

Even though the fear is a normal part of human existence, you need not be constrained or confused. Pause, take a break, and take a breath. Understand the mental and physical dimensions of terror. Let it slow you down, but don't stop you. See the quality of your resources. Rate it. Enjoy it. You built the space for the radiation of your luminous self.

7.1 Life-Changing Facts about Fear

Are you ready to go deep into, to really indulge in the pursuit of freedom from fear, consider joining the intense 3-week Flourish in the Face of Fear? Directly address your anxiety and see if there are any great ways your life doesn't change.

"The appearance of fear is a sure sign that you trust your own power." If you're a human being, you're likely to experience fear. For survival, these bodies in which we live are created, and fear is the gatekeeper. This protects us and keeps us safe and protected by keeping us aware of any potential threat that could come our way. Fear produces caution, watchfulness, and mistrust.

What's perfect if you're chased by a hungry lion? But if your goal is to live in the abundance that is always here, lead with your heart, be open to the depth and breadth of what is possible in your life, then fear is worthy of your attention.

Simply said a Sacred Option, running out of fear does not work. If we do not turn to face it, it will forever nip at our feet. What does it mean? We are living a life of terror, choosing partners, careers, and friends out of fear. Habits and addictions are wild because we are fearful that our needs will be met. We feel isolated and disconnected, though quietly whispering deep inside; we hear the echo of reality.

Facts of Fear

1. All about "can't" are fear-motivated feelings. They create a gloomy, hypothetical future scenario. Here's the truth: you

How to Make Fear your Ally

don't know what will happen, so it's not likely that these thoughts will be real. Buy these ideas, and you're screaming for limits. Let them go on and you're going to see what's really true about you.

2. We are designed to keep you safe and constrained by fearful thoughts. It's not wisdom, it's not reality. You can choose what to do.

3. Fear often involves perceptions of the body. Learn to recognize these and accept them with an open heart as they are. Turn the strength of fear into enthusiasm and excitement.

4. Fear makes us think something bad is going to happen if the fact is, we don't know what's going to happen. Make yourself comfortable with not knowing, so anxiety does not control you.

5. it's enhanced by fighting terror. The cure is mindfulness-able to experience fear explicitly as it happens to you at the moment, knowing the physical sensations and thoughts.

6. The goal is not only to get rid of fear because you don't have the power to do that. But the way you react to fear, you have the power to change. Learn to accept it with curiosity and a loving heart learn how to spin thoughts that deflate your passion for things. But we shouldn't feel like something is wrong or if it fails to occur, you have failed. Just meet it with love every time.

7. After a moment of truth, a wave of fear appears to emerge. Say there's an idea in your mind that you'd love to do something. You will soon notice that your mind is full of excuses why you can't or shouldn't do it. Recognize that it's all about terror.

8. You can make conscious choices by acknowledging the existence of fear. You have the insight to see what fear is driving you to do, and what you really want to do.

9. The enemy is not terror. It may be the voice of reason, prudence, and practicality that sometimes serves you well.

10. That's right. Resisting fear requires energy. Get to know it and allowing the body and mind to relax as the fight is over. It creates a space for imagination, wonder, awe, passion, beauty and inspiration.

Read from anxiety. Know it so well that it will not be able to sneak on you. Stay rid of the chains of terror, and it will shine every moment of your life.

7.2 Five Things We Can Learn from Our Fear

Fear is a sensation most of us are trying to avoid. We should do whatever it takes not to notice a feeling of fear, much less to get closer to it. You could suggest we're afraid.

As Franklin D. Roosevelt famously said, "Fear itself is the only thing we need to fear." What exactly did he mean by that–and why should we care? Through the Great Depression, FDR led the United States. During a time when people rushed to the banks and withdrew money, he spoke. This has contributed to the country's economic crisis. So, FDR basically told people that their anxiety made things worse.

In fact, the FDR closed banks for several days, calling for a special Congress session to give citizens time to calm down and give the country a chance to start making plans for recovery. He admitted that it can potentially be debilitating when fear hits.

There's a lot we can learn from FDR's method of understanding fear, taking the time to calm down, and then choosing the right step. But most of us have not been taught how to understand fear to separate it from doubt, anxiety, or overwhelm more effectively deal with it.

If you think back to a traumatic or anxiety-producing occurrence you've witnessed, you might believe that any mental images you've produced going into it were worse than the actual event itself once you've actually gone through the experience. Maybe by noticing it earlier or by taking a different approach you could have saved a good bit of energy.

Here are five actual things we can learn from our fear:

1. Fear in the Extreme:

In most situations, the thing we fear is never as bad as we think it could be when we feel anxious about something. We're approaching unknown territory when we're trying to make a big decision or embark on something different. Our minds are always trying to keep us safe. That often means avoiding change, even if the situation in which we find ourselves no longer serves us or can hold us back. The essence of such a change means that we may not know what is going to happen on the other side of it. And the unknown may be scary, indeed. If you feel anxious or fearful of a new opportunity or a transition, try to break it down and take smaller steps.

2. Fear as a Signal:

Fear is a strong signal that tells us it's time for a break. When you find that more and more things appear to be scary or even somewhat daunting, it can be a very real sign that your mind and spirit need a break. Take a day off, take off the weekend, and find time for a real holiday. Better still, devote yourself to finding ways to replenish and refresh. How can you manage your time and resources so you can't get back to this stage so quickly?

3. Fear as growth:

 In fact, fear often alerts us to a danger. But often, if we look at it more closely, it's where our greatest opportunity lies on the other side of fear. Try to act in your fear and discomfort. This can be incredibly liberating and inspiring. Clarity, after all, comes from engaging, not talking about engaging. Note that you can always change or adapt, if you think the move wasn't the best, you can even reverse course. It's normal to have some anxiety as we take on something different, rising beyond current boundaries and limitations. Try to make it a bridge rather than a roadblock.

4. Fear as a practice:

Many of us are afraid of failure. And yet we also know that many times have disappointed the most highly successful men. Have you ever tried to do it? Are you allowed to try something you definitely weren't going to succeed? If we struggle or mess up, we always remember that after all, it wasn't all that bad. When you worry too much about taking action in your anxiety, encourage yourself to see a worst-case scenario. Imagine taking the action you fear: make the speech, buy the new office building, and launch your blog. Picture something going wrong and seeing yourself living through it, perhaps even laughing about it–or at least learning from it– down the road. You can find the anxiety subsiding now that you have witnessed the worst-case scenario. Connecting with a more likely outcome and moving past current boundaries and weaknesses may even be simpler.

5. Fear as a Friend:

Anxiety is part of life and there are times when everyone is grappling with it. I'm not saying you're trying to completely eradicate fear. It wouldn't be useful, not only would that be impossible. A calculated amount of fear is actually healthy. Whether you are walking through the woods, starting a new project, or growing a successful business, it's good to be aware and alert. But too much anxiety over a prolonged period of time means that most of the time your body, mind and spirit function in overdrive. It drains energy that you need, makes it harder to make decisions, and ensures that you may ignore red flags alerting you to the real risks that need your attention. When it emerges, be willing to recognize fear, ask what you can learn from it. Try to breathe in or take a walk. So, if you feel more relaxed, ask: is this intuitive advice actually leading you in a better direction? Or maybe it's an old cap and belief that gets you going in a new direction?

If even 10 percent of your anxiety could be magically eliminated, how would you work and life is different? What if you were able to learn to tolerate the rest? Hold it for a moment. If you've been stopped from fulfilling a dream by too much anxiety or worry, practice making your friend fear.

How are you going to embrace the terror this year? How can you be afraid to become an ally as you step forward with that great new idea, develop your company, or have that hard conversation?

7.3 What if fear didn't exist?

Take a moment to reflect on this.

What do you think about it? Unless we didn't face any uncertainties in our lives, would anything ever be done?

These days, we will find many excuses to be afraid. There are many causes of concern from what is happening in the world around us to problems at work and/or at home. You've probably been told not to be afraid of anything all your life. Fear and vulnerability are often associated with it. Fear, we're told, is for cowards.

But sometimes it's nice to fear.

Many others write about terror as well. Hundreds of self-improvement forums can be found that inform you that anxiety is a bad thing. Others might say that fear is preventing people from pursuing their dreams, so to live your dream life you have to remove your fear.

1) Anxiety is a symbol of something amazing you're doing!

Have you got a bucket list? I bet you've put some scary stuff on it, if you do. Why are we trying to do things that are scary?

It's because we know these things are going to make our lives better. Note, when you are scared of your ambitions, that you are seeking something great, something that will survive far beyond the temporary pain that you may feel along the way. Hold the amazing in sight.

2) Anxiety is creating new doors for us!

You lay the foundation for new possibilities when you are afraid of something, but then take the fear by the horns and overcome it, one step at a time. Bravery is a source of bravery. Whether it's starting a new job, running your first marathon, or some other obstacle, the anxiety you experience can be the first inkling of some great new possibilities. Search for it, follow it.

3) Fear starts with us!

What would inspire you in a scary scenario to act? That's a healthy fear. If confronted by us or others we love, we take action, our fear pushes us forward. That push will support every aim you have, driven by fear. We still forget that every day we have power over our own lives, our decisions. To get going, let your fear drive you forward.

4) Anxiety fosters our independence!

Fear holds you in the moment and helps you to capitalize on this very minute's excitement and strength. Even if you leap for just a few seconds from your comfort zone, accepting your terror, you will discover in your universe a new sense of freedom. Hop on. Turn on.

If used in the right way, fear can be very strong. So, what are you thinking about today?

For most of us, anxiety is a constant companion when we go through a challenging time. When they start their drumbeat, it seems almost impossible to stop the "what ifs" in our head. "What if I'm losing my job?"What if I can't take care of my

---

child?"What if I can't make my mortgage or rent?"It may be natural to be scared, but it will leave you helpless and unable to act in order to change your situation.

When anxiety grips the wheel, it's hard to make positive choices and guide yourself in a new direction. I love the fear advice obtained from her intuition by author Sophie Burnham. Throughout her book, The Way of Prayer, she shares it. "Don't worry," the voice said. "You don't have to think! Only relax and let things happen in the right time. Let the law of quiet, calm, and harmony, and prevent stressful situations. Let them be born, live and straighten up happily, not with fear or pressure, but simply by accepting the fact it will succeed if you allow yourself to be guided instead of trying to force things. Everything is perfect and stays fine. "Isn't that incredibly comforting?

Accept Fear

When something becomes daunting and you're frightened, what do you want to do? You're going to run away! If you only had a magic wand to make things go away. You'd like to click on your heels like Dorothy in Oz's Wizard and voila, you're back in Kansas (or wherever safety resides), what else can you do when you're in the icy grip of fear? You should relax and enjoy it.

Fear is never static or any other emotion. It's shifting, moving, going up and down, in and out. If you can just recognize and tolerate terror, it's going to start losing its control over you. If we can look deeply into the thing, we are afraid of, we can change its grip on us instead of running away.

Try this: Ask yourself, "What are you concerned about?"Write down the reply. Tell yourself, "If that thing actually happens that I'm scared of, what am I going to do?"Continue to repeat this exercise until you have depleted your chances of terrifying outcomes. When I do this exercise, what I generally find is that I end up feeling mildly amused by all the unlikely scenarios that my imagination will come up with.

Eleanor Roosevelt, the former first lady, wrote, "You gain strength, courage, and trust from every encounter you really stop looking in front of you for fear. You should say it to yourself. I've witnessed this terror. I 'ill handle the next thing that comes along.' "You're not fighting for fear. It's something in your life that you make room for. Take it up and make it your friend and not your enemy.

Take Action

Anxiety will permeate our mind if we allow it for too long to be pessimistic in there. This takes on its own identity, reminding us of our own inefficiency and worthlessness. Joyce Meyer, a famous speaker and pastor, says, "God does not want us to be afraid. Yet even if we are afraid, we can choose to trust God and take action. "I discovered that faith is the best antidote to fear. If you got immobilized by anxiety, ask yourself, "What one thing I could do today that would make me feels better?"It can be a plain, easy thing or a huge, audacious thing. Your intuition will begin to offer suggestions when you ask a question like this. It could be having coffee with a friend, writing a letter to someone you need to forgive, being brave enough to make a financial planner appointment, seeing a therapist or other professional healer.

Philosopher Ralph Waldo Emerson wrote, "Do whatever you're afraid to do." Trust that the right answer is anything that stimulates your interest or curiosity. Maybe it doesn't make sense, but it does! This is how intuition works. You know or feel nudged about doing something, but often you don't know why!

Freedom is on the other side of all terror. In turn, by taking action, you will find freedom. This helps to get you out of your old thinking, your old way of being, and actions that has partly led to the situation of your current life. Has it accompanied you on your walk instead of struggling with fear while you begin an action path?

The Small Step Action Plan

One Small Step Could Change Your Life be written by Robert Maurer. For anyone having a crisis or just feeling stuck, I think it should be necessary to read. There is no question that his technique is easy. It also taps into your own inner wisdom to provide you with the answers you are looking for and helps you overcome fear and resistance. His theory is that there are small steps that we can all do. Because they are doable and achievable, they add up to big improvements.

1) Ask your little questions. "What could I do differently today if health were my first priority?"

2) Speak of little feelings. Think of a job or circumstance that makes you nervous or uncomfortable. Spend a couple of seconds (not minutes) every day to see a successful outcome.

3) Take small steps. Examples: If your aim is to avoid over-spending, removing one item from your shopping cart before going to the counter could be a small action. If your aim is to better manage your tension, taking a deep breath might be a small step.

4) Small problems to solve. Often you will receive intuitive alerts about an upcoming crisis well in advance of the crisis. Don't ignore the signs of early warning. Talk. Listen. Pay attention to the details you get and act on it.

Eventually, get yourself back to the present moment when you find yourself having anxious feelings about your situation. Keep your mind focused on the many things that you do that you may be grateful for.

Chapter 8: Ways to Think Differently About Fear

When you stand in front of a door that says "fear," that's the door, you have to step through to succeed.

Performance starts right beyond the comfort zone as the adage goes. In peace, there is no fear. When there's protection, there's nothing driving you. There's complacency where there's warmth. Contentment is the perfect counterbalance to performance.

You have to master fear, grasp its real purpose, and use it to your most significant advantage to becoming abundantly prosperous. You will understand you're potential if you learn to fear and how to use it.

1. The challenge of fear

When you're unsure about your next business move, anxiety ignites, and you may fall victim to the illusion that you're putting your company at risk of failure. The initial reaction of being inclined to avoid the challenge is naturally created by fear. Keep in mind that fears are a counterintuitive emotion; fear encourages you to leap forward into the unknown when you want to step back.

Anxiety wants you to fight with it to take it on. Success is about the danger and bold decision-making. If you let the fear encapsulate you, it will draw you into negative fasts and for self-reinforcement, because fear feeds on itself. The more you let your fear stop you, the higher will be your fear, and the harder it will be to act.

If you want something but you are afraid of any potential slip-ups that might happen along the way, the competition is determined by fear and won. Learn to move more efficiently than your terror.

2. Fear as an opportunity

You cannot allow any competitor in the pursuit of success, in life or business, to make you feel so vulnerable that you are filled with doubts that hinder action. Most of the concerns you have are not real threats to your company.

Be open to fear's feelings; let it calm down and find your way back to rational thinking. You are using fear as your motivator and coach once emotionally in charge to drive you through challenging situations.

When you prove that fear is wrong again and again, you grow trust in the character trait. Trust could not rise without fear. You become comfortable by accomplishing things you never before felt you were able to do or achieve consistently and effectively.

When used correctly, fear will move you harder than any other emotion towards success.

3. Fear as a curiosity

Without justification, fear does not appear. There's usually something you're afraid of. Naturally, in the company, thoughts of failure or loss cause you to do everything you can to prevent these encounters. Evasion, however, achieves nothing but a complete breakdown of your imagination, generating mental blocks that hinder progress.

Be curious about what you're afraid of to stop falling victim to terror. If you can work emotionally through what you fear, you have the opportunity to answer for yourself what needs to be done to get out of this negative state and use its strength to your advantage.

4. Fear to direct you

Fear creates an unconscious state of heightened anxiety that causes you to turn in and pay close attention when faced with life or business challenges. Anxiety warns you when you have to be vigilant, and when you have to be brave in making your decisions.

Fear is a friend of good sense, so listen to his voice. Occasionally anxiety will tell you, "It's now or never," and sometimes it will say to you, "Sleep on it, give it time." These are your guidebooks to compromise and prepare your next move.

5. Fear is as useful as that

It's not good or bad, it's just uncomfortable. There's no need to go broader than that. It will stifle your development when you allow fearing the unreasonable power to paralyse you.

Imagine if you have treated fear as you have handled any other emotion. You will come to understand its utility in learning to do this and be more able to harness its power proactively. You'd come to see that fear is perhaps the most valuable tool used to achieve your goals.

It helps you to see the apparent benefit of fear driving the evolution of yourself and your company as you equate fear with potential (a positive experience). You come to respect fear as the gateway to your increased prosperity, satisfaction, and fulfilment as you experience the joy of going beyond fear.

For this reason, always remember that on the other side of fear, there is everything you want.

6. Fear as well as experience

Fear is closely associated with the intestine. Although this feeling can be painful, it gives you the tough love that you don't normally graciously embrace from others. When you get the best of your thoughts and emotions, you're forced to listen.

Flow-through your emotional state to use this insight to intuit the next move outside of your comfort zone to use fear effectively. You become the most effective wisdom teachers driving your business decisions as you learn to master fearful emotions.

You must do the things you're afraid you can't. You are seasoned, knowledgeable, and unrestricted in your progress through this process.

7. Fear of being a catalyst

When you understand why you're concerned about something, it's easier to manage anxiety. When it comes to chasing your dreams, it's natural to be afraid of being "too bold" or "too special." Never under the umbrella of social acceptance and fitting in, take care to stifle your greatness.

Be real. Be bold enough to be you in a competitive business environment where everyone wants to be someone else to keep up with the Jones's. There is no other one with your uniqueness. No one else can do your part, so show your distinctive character.

Transparency is a catalyst for progress. The more honest you are, the less scared you will be different, the more chances you will have to move your way. Enable yourself to be weak and risky. Learn from the powerful emotion of fear to create it incredible.

It's a cause for terror. Let it drive you to be better.

It's natural to feel fear as a human being. Fear in life and industry is a great competitor and motivator. It is the motivation inside you that has the most excellent opportunity to force you to step forward and change. On a very initial level, fear protects you from danger. Still, most of the anxiety that you experience as a human being is the fear of what has not yet happened and the worst-case scenarios that are unlikely ever to happen. Repressed fear produces the unhealthy state of chronic anxiety that rips off any chance of developing the development you need to get you to the kind of steep success you deserve.

You would stop and look fear in the face through every encounter that you open new doors to success.

Chapter 9: Transforming Fear into Your Ally

Instead of going to war in fear and thinking it a failure or question that you have to remove, alter, or transcend the invitation is to respond to it. For millions of years, anxiety has been programmed into your nervous system, and spiritual cycle is unlikely to be reversed in a few decades. You should rest in the strong likelihood that for the rest of your life, in some form or another, fear can emerge most every day. Welcome to this case. You're still alive.

See your current experience very carefully. Is it a question of fear? Is the explosion of emotion, feeling, and strength inside you something that you must continue to argue, blame, and submit to self-aggression movement? Do you have to keep telling stories about how it is the "opposite" of love (as if love had an "opposite") and that as soon as you are no longer afraid, you can turn up and participate completely in your own weakness in life, in relationships?

Is the presence of fear, in fact, the cause of your struggle and suffering? The wavelike feeling feel movement, tearing through your butt, stomach, arms, and shoulders? Or does the pain arise as it passes through you from the loss and rejection of life? As well as the unexamined assumption that its mere presence is evidence of a problem that must be solved as a matter of importance, that something is wrong with you, and that you have failed?

Yeah, fear may be a burning and fierce friend, but it's not an enemy from outside. It's a forgotten part of you calling for your help, coming up here in the radiant, and now to reveal something you've lost contact with.

You will join your fear with practice, and infuse it with your presence, tenderness, interest, and comfort. Also opening your heart to your fear, making friends with your fear. This is, of course, a revolutionary invitation for the mind to accept a difficult time. In a society that has left the shadow in its rush to get to "happiness" at all costs, it is also one that may not go over so well.

But you can begin to open up your anxiety as an act of self-love. Next, drop the word "fear" because the unparalleled energy and color revolution inside you can never be affected. Surround it with your consciousness. And just begin to move a little closer. And see, you know. Close enough to get acquainted with this part of you, but not so close as to integrate and identify with it as who you are, or overpower yourself. Little by little. Short time frames. Two seconds, one second. Three seconds from now. And there's plenty. And then for four or five, maybe next time. Then you have to rest.

Then you may come to learn that the energy movement we call "fear" is not an enemy operating against you, but an ally, sent to bring you closer to yourself and to reveal wholeness. The only way we'll ever know the truth of fearlessness is by being willing to remain embodied in waves of fear.

You can call off the war and put down your dissociating, hostile, and abandoning weapons. Reality will sometimes appear as fear, for even fear in the arms of love as it has its way here is a weapon of skillful means. Slow down, slow down. Say yes to what's going on and it's going to free your mind. The enemy is here. There's nothing that works against you. Only further disclosure. Everywhere is the road.

9.1 Make Fear Your Friend and It Will Do Great Things for You

Fear will really be our friend on the plus side. It can teach us a lot of things. It can be a real game-changer to learn to understand when it happens, and even to accept it as we move on.

We are afraid of failure, reputations destroyed, and even success. We're afraid to talk about our worries in order to top it off.

Of course, fear is not evil in itself. In reality, it can be highly motivating and safe. Fear makes us wary about risky decisions: it fills us with energy and excitement, it drives us forward and it fosters creativity. Fear can be a great ally and friend in the intensely competitive start-up world.

Many of my co-workers had been experts of their fields for decades while I worked for Google as a student. I was afraid I would not live up to their expectations, but I was taught by the experience to face my anxiety, live with it, and master it.

Here are five forms of apprehension that you can become friends:

1. Take it up

You're not a super-human or a robot. Taking into account each day's choices, obligations and threats, fear is a normal response so accept it. If you think positively about terror, instead of a weakness, it becomes a driving force.

Fear will allow you to exert self-control in moderation; it keeps us from making rash decisions. For example, a business leader considering buying a nice-to-have item or service might be afraid that he or she will waste cash at an unnecessary cost. And that's good: Anxiety can provide some sort of gut check to get us to think about big decisions twice.

2. Use paralysis research

Fear will paralyze you and keep you from thinking rationally about the issues at hand. Don't let terror in the corner of the room become a dark monster; examine it. Ask questions like, "If our time line is too short, is this project scary for me?"Solve one piece at a time of the puzzle. A sure way to correct the anxiety is to break down things into separate parts.

3. Manage your own strain

There are different ways in which fear affects people. Past experiences, personality characteristics, and support systems will all impact how we manage heat. But the great news is that being challenged is safe meeting confrontations and tight deadlines helps us to believe in ourselves when we may not instantly. Fear helps us to cope effectively with stress: we are either forced to take up the challenge or let it overtake us.

4. Find your network support

When you have friends on your side, everything is less scary. Surround yourself with trustworthy colleagues and counselors whenever the path gets bumpy you can look at. If your closest allies say you're feeling stressed or recommending a break, believe them. When you feel weak, this support network will act as a mirror. Understanding that you're not alone is soothing and energizing; there's always a gang behind you to fall back on.

5. Know the root cause of your problem

Most business leaders are dealing with anxiety and uncertainty because the root of an issue is difficult to identify. Leaders eventually realize with practice that there are three root causes of problems: individuals, goods, or processes.

The first step is not to panic. Look at the real issue at hand — it may not be as terrifying as you think it is. First, stop rearranging the entire organization to deal with a small problem. Alternatively, take a closer look at the interpersonal actions of your team, the functionality of your product, or the process flow. Find the source of the problem and you're going to be a step closer to a successful resolution.

Everyone is scared, but by recognizing the source of your fear and using it to do your best work, you can set yourself apart from the crowd. The more you embrace fear and learn to respect it, the better you can use it to overwhelm yourself.

Learn How to Make Fear Your Ally

Trying to control the various aspects of life is human nature, but fear is often allowed to wrest control away. Why do you offer this kind of control over your life? Isn't it time to stop letting fear stop you from doing, being, or doing what you want? It's time to face it head-on and push through it when anxiety holds you off from what you really want. How is it possible to overcome fear? Honestly, it's not as hard as it might look at first.

First, please realize that fear is nothing more than the presence of False Evidence True! Understanding its wrong is the secret to turning the power back to you and having the ball back in your hand. The thing that moves you to take "action" to face your fear, to bring it to light, and to dissipate its power. Trust is built up and fear is turned into anticipation, taking you far closer to success.

There are five steps that must be taken, from afraid to courageous, to break the barrier:

1. Recognize apprehension or fear. Make sure you are aware of the situation as a whole. It's not unusual for more than one fear to be at the root of a problem, or a fear that has resurfaced with a new one for a long time.

2. Describe what you're holding back from being, doing, or having anything you're looking for. You must need to have a good understanding of what needs to be done to be able to fight it effectively.

if you didn't have that anxiety, decide what you'd do. Visualize what your life is going to be like if there were no such albatross. How are you going to feel? How many more chances are there for you? How many more stories would there have been? How much happier do you want to be?

3. Identify times when you were faced with apprehension and pushed beyond it successfully.

Everyone can recognize circumstances with a little thought in order to reach a desired result where they step beyond fear. A fear of change (new relationship, new job, graduation, marriage, etc.) where you met and triumphed your dragon! Perhaps a little corny, but you're going to get the gist! Use these moments as touchstones to remind you that you can do this again.

4. Recognize the characteristics that have motivated you to succeed. These are the attributes on which your success is based, and usually the cornerstone for you as an individual. Qualities like tenacity, honesty, passion, confidence, and, to name a few, being able to see the big picture.

So, how do you combat your fears? How do you take off your life's Pause button? What attributes did you draw on in the past to conquer your doubts and fulfill your dreams? It's the time now. Again, take control of your life.

5. Try to concentrate on the final outcome-the success! Using visualization to get to the place where you feel how wonderful it is, how good you are, how simple it is, and how happy it is for you. So, you can stop thinking about fear as your enemy, knowing that it is only false evidence that appears to be true, and accepting it as an ally!

Fear is my ally

Fearlessness is not only the absence of fear, but the capacity remains with one's fear and makes wise use of one's resources. Sunada discusses how dealing with our fears (as opposed to fighting) will lead us to our own position of freedom.

As a bad thing, we tend to think of terror. There's something in our way. After all, one of the Buddha's illuminated virtues is fearlessness. Does this not mean that we should strive to remove fear from our experience?

Not so fast!

Let's remember what anxiety is. At one point, when we are in danger, it's the instinct that propels us to run. Speak of lions and bears running away from the caveman. Adrenaline that pounds the muscle.

When we tone down the strength of fearful energy and strip away our belief that it is "evil," we find an underlying motivator underneath it for positive and thoughtful interaction with our environment.

Now let's turn the pressure down to normal daily levels and get rid of the dreaded snap. It may help to picture the same caveman wandering through the woods without being hunted, but still having to be alert. What are the basic values at stake here? I think he would be mentally conscious, responsive and completely sensitive to all his senses. He is also physically alert quick and ready to respond to any new sights and sounds quickly and appropriately. He'd be conscious and focused in his mind. He's in the moment, and able to apply any of his intellectual quiver's skills and knowledge. He is engaged in his feeling and intuition. He's in a readiness not to the point of hyper-anxiety but a simple, concentrated alertness that can cleverly respond to whatever comes along his way.

I can say that these attributes are the gifts that we are offered through terror. If he had nothing to fear the caveman, he would have no desire to be so keenly interested. He would just be blundering through the bush, losing himself and doing anything. So, if we tone down the strength of fearful energy and strip away our belief that it is "evil," we find an underlying motivator underneath it to interact with our environment consciously and intelligently. It also has the ability to exploit our internal resources that we may not even know about. It is a force capable of moving us forward.

The bad thoughts about terror are what we are really afraid of, not the source of fear itself.

Fear is not so much about physical danger in our present society. Most of us are not constantly met with physical assaults like that caveman. For us, fears are mostly psychological in nature such as taking a leap into a new job or relationship, or fear of isolation, or lack of money. But in fact, all fear is the same.

We've been so over-sold in our collective belief that fear is "evil" that it's turned into an obstacle. Of course, we all experience fear time to time, and yes, it's very unpleasant. Yet we believe that our negative thoughts about fear are what we are really afraid of, not the source of fear itself. We fear it so much that we try to run away from it in our stomach an instinctive reaction from our caveman days. But we are unable to run away from ourselves. It's not just pointless, it's self-defeating too.

 If we have a specific concern that comes up regularly for us, it means that we are facing a wall that we feel is preventing us.

How to Make Fear your Ally

If we have a specific concern that comes up regularly for us, I think it means that we are facing a wall that we feel is preventing us. We're at a border and on the other hand, we know there's equality. If that thing on the other hand were not so important to us, the emotional charge would not be there. Yet going there doesn't feel safe. And the more we try to fight our terror, the more we are welcomed by it. It fills our minds and our emotions are determined. We have been left immobilized and trapped in the same small old place. There's an adage that goes with something like "what we're concentrating on is what's rising." That's another example of that concept.

How if we used it intelligently instead of battling our terror, like that caveman walking through the woods? Unless we feel fear in that moment, we're not in any real danger, are we? Pause, take a breath, and be afraid. Recognize it for what it really is our desire for freedom when we experience that emotional charge. It is something that needs to be accepted, nurtured and loved. Let's be smart to use it.

If listen to fear, it tells us where we need to go in no uncertain terms.

And stick with it when the temperature of fear is rising. But don't struggle against it or indulge in it. Recognize every image of the doomsday that comes up for what it is just feelings. Look at what is really calling for your attention in that moment, with your heightened awareness. What can we do to move forward? As we sit, listening attentively to our terror, we are slowly loosening its grip on us. And gradually, in a smart and grounded way, we develop our trust to really move through to the other side.

When we listen to it, it tells me where we need to go in no uncertain terms. It's not just any useful path, but the exact place we need to break through the most. The flip side of the same coin of terror is either the Buddha's bravery or fearlessness. Interestingly, the more we accept my anxiety, the more we interact with the little wisps of bravery that we find in us.

10. Conclusion

In conclusion, we are all faced with fear. Our fears come either from our insecurity, or from past experiences. We all experience fear and go through it. Some of us use different methods to overcome what we fear. Victoria ends up overcoming her fear by her methods of seeing a syringe every day. She finally had no fear of being treated, and she was not afraid of syringes for a long time. We were shown in the performance that many people are afraid of simple things and that they can be confronted with these things. It may not be the simplest thing to do to face the anxiety, but it may be something you have to do.

Any choice you make in fear requires more fear. Power comes from fear. Liberty is free from fear.

Face your fears and be brave enough to do what scares you. It's not easy to do and it's a frightening thought, isn't it?

When you withhold your focus from terror, what you are really doing is to stop feeding it. And, of course, if something doesn't get cooked, it's gone. In your energy field, it cannot support itself and it will be dismantled.

There will be plenty of distractions as you journey down your own path to happiness, success and wealth. There are going to be a heck of real threats. Some are going to be dangerous while others are going to be the result of your fearful thinking. In these cases, what you need to concentrate on is the confidence you need to use the bravery to do what scares you.

Here's the good news: since I can at least understand mentally that the root of all anxiety is being thought, I don't have to do much out of fear. I don't have to hide things that seem to be uncomfortable or "feel the fear and do it anyway."

11.References

1.   Brown, J. (2017). *We fear death, but what if dying isn't as bad as we think.* [online] the Guardian. Available at: https://www.theguardian.com/science/blog/2017/jul/25/we-fear-death-but-what-if-dying-isnt-as-bad-as-we-think.

2.   HelpGuide.org. (2016). *Social Anxiety Disorder.* [online] Available at: https://www.helpguide.org/articles/anxiety/social-anxiety-disorder.htm.

3.   Thriveglobal.com. (2018). *5 Ways to Distinguish Between Negative and Positive Fear - Thrive Global.* [online] Available at: https://thriveglobal.com/stories/5-ways-to-distinguish-between-negative-and-positive-fear/.

4.   Thriveglobal.com. (2019). *5 Ways to Distinguish Between Negative and Positive Fear - Thrive Global.* [online] Available at: https://thriveglobal.com/stories/5-ways-to-distinguish-between-negative-and-positive-fear/.

5.   Thriveglobal.com. (2019). *5 Ways to Distinguish Between Negative and Positive Fear - Thrive Global.* [online] Available at: https://thriveglobal.com/stories/5-ways-to-distinguish-between-negative-and-positive-fear/.

6.   Effective-mind-control.com. (2019). *What Causes Fear.* [online] Available at: https://www.effective-mind-control.com/what-causes-fear.html.

7.   Spiritualjourney17.com. (2019). *Freedom from Fear – Conclusion.* [online] Available at: https://spiritualjourney17.com/2016/01/21/is-fear-real-part-ii/.